The Carer's Guide to Schizophrenia

of related interest

Can't You Hear Them?
The Science and Significance of Hearing Voices
Simon McCarthy-Jones
ISBN 978 1 78592 256 5
eISBN 978 1 78450 541 7

Hearing Voices, Living Fully
Living with the Voices in My Head
Claire Bien
Foreword by Larry Davidson
ISBN 978 1 78592 718 8
eISBN 978 1 78450 322 2

The Patient Revolution
How We Can Heal the Healthcare System
David Gilbert
ISBN 978 1 78592 538 2
eISBN 978 1 78450 932 3

The Carer's Guide to
SCHIZOPHRENIA

A Concise, Problem-Solving
Resource for Family and Friends

Terence V. McCann, Dan I. Lubman
and Gayelene Boardman

Foreword by Professor Allan Fels

Jessica Kingsley Publishers
London and Philadelphia

First published in Great Britain in 2021 by Jessica Kingsley Publishers

An Hachette Company

2

Copyright © Terence V. McCann, Dan I. Lubman and Gayelene Boardman 2021
Foreword copyright © Professor Allan Fels 2021

A CIP catalogue record for this title is available from the
British Library and the Library of Congress

ISBN 978 1 78775 504 8
eISBN 978 1 78775 505 5

Printed and bound by CPI Group (UK) Ltd, Croydon, CR0 4YY

Jessica Kingsley Publishers' policy is to use papers that are natural, renewable and recyclable products and made from wood grown in sustainable forests. The logging and manufacturing processes are expected to conform to the environmental regulations of the country of origin.

Jessica Kingsley Publishers
73 Collier Street
London N1 9BE, UK

www.jkp.com

Contents

Foreword

Schizophrenia has a devastating effect on people with the illness and their families. It is a roller-coaster and unpredictable illness and has similar consequences for the challenges it places on families. It is associated with emotional, physical and financial hardship, with families frequently experiencing a contrasting range of emotions as they struggle to comprehend what is happening to their loved one.

With the right support, people with schizophrenia can lead fulfilling and satisfying lives. Simultaneously, families can begin the process of coming to terms with their loved one's illness. For some families, the onset of the illness enhances existing good relationships with the individual. Other families may not have had such close relationships, and even though the illness presents challenges, it can help unite families in a closer, more open and profound relationship than before.

The unique and ongoing contribution of families in supporting the individual with schizophrenia is frequently taken for granted and undervalued, and they are often excluded from treatment discussions by mental health professionals. Moreover, families often experience a gap in service provision in meeting their own needs as well as that of the person with schizophrenia. This is an important consideration, because positive family coping and being optimistic about the future wellbeing of the person with schizophrenia—that things will improve, eventually—are associated with better outcomes for families and the individual.

I write this foreword from the dual perspectives of having a family member with schizophrenia and from long-standing professional experience in the governance of organizations in the mental health field. In 1996, my eldest daughter, Isabella, was diagnosed with schizophrenia at the age of 25 years. Because of the high-profile and public nature of my work at that time (I was chairman of the Australian Competition and Consumer Commission, the nation's corporate watchdog), I kept Isabella's diagnosis a secret for fear that it would be used against me. From a professional perspective, I am a director of MIND Australia, one of the country's leading community-managed specialist psychosocial mental health service providers. I am Board member of The Haven Foundation, a subsidiary of MIND Australia, which provides accommodation and daily living support for socially and financially disadvantaged people living with mental illness. I am also a former Chair of the Australian National Mental Health Commission, the peak body with responsibility for monitoring and reporting on investment in mental health and suicide prevention initiatives, providing evidence-based policy advice to the Government and disseminating information on ways to continuously improve Australia's mental health and suicide prevention systems, and acting as a catalyst for change to achieve those improvements. Currently I am a Commissioner of the Victorian Royal Commission on Mental Health. Taken together, my personal and professional experiences have given me a unique and profound insight into, and understanding of, the devastating effect of mental illness on the affected individual and their families, as well as the needs of families in this situation.

The authors of *The Carer's Guide to Schizophrenia: A Concise, Problem-Solving Resource for Family and Friends* (Terence McCann, Dan Lubman and Gayelene Boardman) are passionate in their commitment to improving the quality of life for people with schizophrenia and their families. In particular, McCann and Lubman have conducted several studies into the experience of families and caregivers in the mental health and substance use fields. *The Carer's Guide to Schizophrenia* is based on their previous research into families. I highlight five key features of the book in helping families cope in supporting a member with schizophrenia. First, it is a practical and easy-to-read book, and can be read in full or in part. Second, it addresses most of the major challenges that families face in supporting a member (or friend) with schizophrenia and contains a focus on families looking after their own wellbeing. Third, it adopts a problem-solving approach, an objective and flexible framework for dealing with day-to-day issues associated with support-giving. Fourth, it places emphasis on working cooperatively with, and valuing, the family member with schizophrenia. Fifth, the book has been written to an international readership—in developed and developing countries—and contains a helpful list of country-specific Internet resources for families in a wide range of countries.

Overall, *The Carer's Guide to Schizophrenia* is a valuable resource for helping families support a loved one with schizophrenia.

Professor Allan Fels, PhD, AO
University of Melbourne, Australia

Acknowledgements

We would like to thank the following members of the Carer Expert Advisory Group for their helpful suggestions and insightful reviews of the book:

- Dr Margaret Leggatt, PhD, independent mental health care professional, Melbourne, Australia.

- Sheree Hollywood, Mental Illness Fellowship, North Queensland, Australia.

- Margaret Doherty, Mental Health Matters 2, Perth, Australia.

- Judith Evans, Carer Consultant, Midwest Area Mental Health Service, Melbourne, Australia.

We would also like to thank the following members of the Content Expert Advisory Group for reviewing the book and for their excellent suggestions:

- Professor Christine Barrowclough, Professor of Clinical Psychology, University of Manchester, Manchester, UK.

- Kingsley Crisp, Senior Case Manager, Orygen Youth Health, Melbourne, Australia.

- Professor Alan Simpson, Professor of Mental Health Nursing, Kings College, London, UK.

- Professor David Castle, Chair of Psychiatry, St Vincent's Health and the University of Melbourne, Melbourne, Australia.

Our thanks also to Judith Johnston for her excellent contribution to writing earlier drafts of the book and to the writing of the self-help manual for the study; and to Betty Kitchener and Professor Anthony Jorm, PhD, for giving us permission to include some parts of their Mental Health First Aid program in this guide.[1] We would also like to thank Meg Polacsek for her editorial assistance in later drafts of the book.

---

[1] www.mhfa.com.au

We would also like to thank the following people who made helpful suggestions about the internet contacts for carers, family and friends in the countries listed in the Appendix:

- Dr Tim Bradshaw, PhD, Reader in Mental Health Nursing, University of Manchester, Manchester, UK.

- Dr Allison Crowe, PhD, Associate Professor, East Carolina University, Greenville, USA.

- Dr Ingrid Daniels, PhD, Director, Cape Mental Health, Cape Town, South Africa.

- Professor Kim Foster, PhD, Professor of Mental Health at Northwestern Mental Health and Australian Catholic University, Melbourne, Australia.

- Dr Penny MacCourt, PhD, Healthwell Educators and Consultants Ltd, Nanaimo, Canada.

- Dr Anthony O'Brien, PhD, Senior Lecturer, University of Auckland, Auckland, New Zealand.

- Dr Jacqui O'Riordan, PhD, Lecturer, University College Cork, Cork, Ireland.

- Professor Wai Tong Chien, PhD, The Chinese University of Hong Kong, Hong Kong SAR.

Our appreciation also to Janssen-Cilag for providing us with an educational grant to support the writing of the book.

Finally, we would like to thank Orygen Youth Health and the Recovery and Prevention of Psychosis Service, both situated in Melbourne, for giving us permission to recruit carer participants from their services for the initial study upon which the book is based, and the Australian Rotary Health Research Fund for funding the study. We also thank the case managers at both services and the carer support program at Orygen for assistance with recruitment. Our sincere appreciation too for the contribution of the co-investigators in the study (listed alphabetically): Dr Helen Baker, Lisa Catania, Eileen Clark, Professor Sue Cotton, Kingsley Crisp, Belinda Dimmock, Professor John Gleeson, Dr Claudia Marck, Flora McCann and Professor Brendan Murphy. Moreover, we would like to thank the carer participants and their families for their invaluable contribution to the study.

Disclaimer

The information contained in this book is not intended to replace the services of trained medical professionals or to be a substitute for medical advice. You are advised to consult a doctor on any matters relating to your health, and in particular on any matters that may require diagnosis or medical attention. The book is sold or otherwise distributed on the condition that the authors and copyright holders and others involved in its production and distribution shall not be liable for any loss or damage suffered from any actions taken as a result of information or opinions contained in it.

— CHAPTER 1 —

Introduction

Purpose of the book

The Carer's Guide to Schizophrenia: A Concise, Problem-Solving Resource for Family and Friends has been written to help carers, family members and friends understand their role and equip them with the skills to cope with and support a person with schizophrenia. Providing support to a person with schizophrenia can be challenging and demanding, but also highly rewarding.

The book focuses on supporting a person with schizophrenia, but people who are supporting a person with other psychoses may find it helpful too.

The book describes aspects of schizophrenia, types of treatment available, how to deal with problems, promoting the person's wellbeing, strengthening the carer's wellbeing, and getting help from support services. It has been structured to provide you with information and, through a series of problem-solving activities, help you review what you have learnt and practice what to do in certain situations. Some of these activities and key messages are repeated throughout the book. This is intended to help you become an experienced problem solver and to reinforce important messages that may help you in your important supportive role.

Reading this book will assist you in your role as a carer. There may be times when you are working through it that you find yourself overwhelmed by the information or activities. This is normal. You can take a break and come back to it later. Most importantly, remember to reward yourself, for example spending some time with friends or by yourself.

Family members and supportive friends may also like to read this book, as many of the issues they encounter are similar to those a carer may experience. It may help them better understand the disorder and what the person they are supporting is going through.

Throughout the book, the term "health professional" is used to refer to the case manager, psychiatrist, medical doctor (general practitioner or GP), or member of a mental health team (mental health nurse, psychologist, social worker, occupational therapist). It refers to who is responsible for the person's overall health care and treatment.

The role of the carer

A carer is a person who provides help and support to someone with a medical or mental health problem. The term "carer" is commonly used to describe family members or friends who provide voluntary support, rather than paid professionals or care workers who are employed to provide a service. A carer may be a family member of the person being cared for, a friend or a neighbor. They may live with the person or live apart.

It is important for the carer to become highly knowledgeable about the person's mental health problem, how it affects them and how best to help in different situations. Carers may provide emotional and practical support and encourage the person to seek appropriate support and treatment. Carers may become involved in treatment plans and, above all, make the person feel supported, needed and loved. Major roles include monitoring the person's mental state, watching for signs of relapse, supporting their wellbeing and encouraging them to take their medication and attend medical appointments. Carers do not always realize that they also need to spend time looking after their own wellbeing.

Being a support person can be a stressful and demanding role, and carers are sometimes required to cope and look after someone else when they themselves feel exhausted, isolated, stressed or ill. Chapter 5 deals with these issues and tries to help you develop skills to look after yourself better.

Throughout your time as a carer, try to:

- Look after yourself: even if you do not think so, you are the most important person in your life.

- Have realistic expectations about what you can do: you will face many challenges in your role, and you may have to make difficult choices.

- Ask for help from as many people as possible, for example family members, friends, neighbors or support services.

- Not be afraid of prioritizing your own needs: it is okay for you to go out and enjoy yourself or have a break.

- Find someone to talk to: it can be particularly useful to talk to professionals such as a health professional or a counselor, other people who are in a similar situation to you such as a carer support group, an educational support group, or close friends or family.

Throughout your time as a carer, and by using this book, you will develop many skills to equip you with looking after yourself and the person you are supporting, and to access and get support from mental health services. These are valid and important skills that will help the person throughout their disorder and beyond. Do not think of yourself as "just a carer"—your role is essential and highly important.

Communicating with health professionals

As a carer, you are highly likely to come into contact with health professionals. For some carers, it is a relatively straightforward process to meet with and develop a working relationship with these professionals. For others, it may be a more challenging prospect. Furthermore, you may have to renew your working relationships with health professionals many times. Services often have frequent changes of staff, or the person with schizophrenia, their family or carers may relocate, making it necessary for them to engage with another mental health service.

If you have difficulty discussing personal or emotional problems with the health professional, this is the first obstacle you may have to consider overcoming. By overcoming this difficulty, you may be in a better position to get the best care and treatment for the person with schizophrenia and for yourself. Being able to communicate openly with health professionals and support services will assist you greatly in your caring role.

In communicating with health professionals, please be aware that these professionals may be hesitant to engage with you because of perceived issues associated with patient confidentiality. Even though the professional is bound by confidentiality, they can still listen to your concerns and provide assistance and support.

You can try to overcome communication difficulties by:

- Understanding that confidentiality laws may bind the health professionals you are communicating with. They cannot tell anyone about your situation or the person's situation, unless it is to another health professional dealing with the person's case, or if the person is at risk of harming themselves or others.

- Trying to concentrate on the positive aspects of being able to communicate freely with health professionals, such as having a close and trusting relationship and being able to understand each other better.

- Reminding yourself that you will be able to assist and support the person you are supporting better if you can communicate openly with health professionals and representatives of support services.

Communicating with health professionals (and other service providers) is discussed further in Chapter 9.

Relationships with family and friends

Relationships with family and friends may change when a family member is developing or experiencing schizophrenia. In this book, the term "family" includes spouses, partners, siblings (brothers and sisters), children (young and old) and other relatives. Family and friends may feel frustration, disappointment, disbelief, anger, confusion, blame or shame when coming to terms with the fact that their family member or friend is unwell. Grief and loss may also be involved, as family and friends feel the person's former personality and achievements have been affected by the disorder.

When a person is recovering from schizophrenia, family and friends can play an important role in helping their relative or friend recover. They can provide love, stability, dignity, respect, understanding, reassurance and support, as well as help with practical issues.

It will be helpful if family members also read this book. However, they may find it overwhelming to read about the things they could do to look after the person. It often takes time for everyone to adjust to what they have learnt. Try not to worry—over time you will all become more experienced at providing better care for the person.

Overall, seeking help from family and friends will assist you in your support role. Perhaps a small group of family and friends could share the role with you, and together you can help the person towards recovery.

Background to the book

This book is based on the authors' previous self-help manual *Reaching Out: Supporting a Family Member or Friend with First-Episode Psychosis*. The effectiveness of the self-help manual was tested as part of a large study that was funded by the Australian Rotary Health Research Fund. Carers of young people experiencing a first episode of psychosis were recruited into the study and randomly divided into two groups. One group received the self-help manual, while the other group did not. People in both groups received a brief encouraging telephone call each week. The results of the study showed that carers who were provided with the self-help manual had a better experience when supporting a family member or friend than those who did not. These effects continued over the three months of the study and were still apparent ten weeks later. By the end of the study, these carers also experienced a greater reduction in unhelpful attitudes about having to provide extra support to the young person experiencing a first episode of psychosis. The level of psychological distress (unpleasant emotions or feelings that interfere with carers' day-to-day functioning) also decreased at a greater rate in those receiving the manual.

At the end of the study, carers were asked to evaluate the usefulness of the self-help manual. Overall, they felt the manual was helpful in promoting their own wellbeing and that it helped increase their understanding of and support for the young person with first-episode psychosis. They also found that the content and book format of the manual were very convenient.

Overview of chapters

Chapter 2:

- Definition of schizophrenia and description of what the person you are supporting may be experiencing.

- Different phases of schizophrenia, types of symptoms and possible causes.

- Myths, stereotypes and stigma associated with the disorder.

Chapter 3:

- Types of treatment involved in schizophrenia.

- Medication and psychosocial treatments, such as stress management, family therapy, support groups, social and life skills training, psychological therapies, psychoeducation and mindfulness.

- The *Hearing Voices* and *Open Dialogue* approaches.

Chapter 4:

- The concept of using problem-solving skills to deal with the problems that carers experience as part of their role.

- Review of problem-solving abilities.

- Introduction to the ADAPT problem-solving framework.

From Chapter 5 onwards, an ADAPT problem-solving or "review and reflect" exercise is provided at the end of each chapter. The problem-solving exercises are opportunities to practice your problem-solving skills relevant to the topic of that chapter, while the "review and reflect" exercises encourage you to review the topic and reflect on what you would do in certain situations.

Chapter 5:

- Looking after your own health and mental wellbeing.
- Information on skills and coping methods that you can use.
- The roles of family and friends and older carers.
- How to challenge the myths, stereotypes and stigma associated with schizophrenia.

Chapter 6:

- Improving the person's health and wellbeing.
- The importance of helpful family support.
- Information on stress management techniques, impaired awareness, reluctance to take medication, and what recovery and relapse mean.

Chapters 7 and 8 are designed for young carers, and carers from different cultures, respectively. They may not be relevant to all readers.

Chapter 7:

- Who young carers are and the challenges they face.
- How young carers can best look after themselves, get support and come to terms with their feelings and emotions.
- A reminder that they are not responsible for the person's disorder.

Chapter 8:

- The challenges of supporting the person when there are cultural and language differences when dealing with the mental health service.
- How to get support from services and family.

Chapter 9:

- How the carer can best get support from mental health services.
- Information on carers' rights and responsibilities.
- Confidentiality law.
- How to communicate with service providers and make complaints.

Chapter 10:

- The importance of effective communication between the carer and the person.
- How best the carer can communicate with them, particularly during difficult periods.
- The concept of "expressed emotion," which describes how communication within the family can affect the person's path to recovery.

In Chapters 11 to 18, the specific problems and symptoms of schizophrenia that carers regularly have difficulty dealing with are discussed.

Chapter 11:

- Depression and how the carer and the person may experience it.
- Information on the types and symptoms of depression, and various treatments.

Chapter 12:

- The problems that occur when the person has reduced motivation, withdraws socially or experiences sleep problems.
- How you can help the person manage these problems.

Chapter 13:

- How the person may exhibit risky behavior.
- Examples of the types of risky behavior.
- The link between risky and vulnerable behavior.
- Ways of working with the person to prevent this behavior.

Chapter 14:

- What the person is experiencing when they are having hallucinations or delusions.
- Information on ways to help the person when they are experiencing these symptoms.
- The *Hearing Voices* approach.

Chapter 15:

- The risk of weight gain for people with schizophrenia.

- How supporting the person to maintain a healthy diet and exercise routine can help them address any weight gain issues.

Chapter 16:

- The occurrence of aggressive behavior in people with schizophrenia.

- Information on how the person can manage their anger.

- How to help prevent and respond to their aggressive behavior.

- The importance of identifying triggers to aggressive behavior.

Chapter 17:

- The harmful effects of substance use for people with schizophrenia.

- How people can be recognized as having a substance use and mental health problem.

- Information on harm minimization and how you can help the person overcome their problem.

Chapter 18:

- The risk of suicide for people with schizophrenia.

- Warning signs of suicide and how to respond to these signs.

- What to do in an emergency.

- Information on self-harm, how to watch for signs of self-harming and how best to respond to these signs.

Chapter 19:

- The recovery principles and the definitions of recovery.

- Examples of what may happen to the person in the future.

- How you can continue to look after your own health and wellbeing.

A guide to getting the most from the book

Each carer has their own unique knowledge, expertise and needs about supporting the person with schizophrenia. Therefore, you need to take this into consideration when setting out to read this book. For some carers who have a great deal of knowledge and experience in the caring role, the book may serve as a useful reference, where you can read relevant chapters that are most appropriate to your needs. In this situation, we recommend you begin by reading Chapter 4 and then choose the most relevant chapter to your needs. For carers who are relatively new to the caring role, we suggest you begin at Chapter 2 and then read each subsequent chapter in the order in which it is presented. Thereafter, the book may serve as a useful reference, where you can read the chapter that best suits your needs.

CHAPTER 2

Understanding Schizophrenia

What is schizophrenia?

This chapter introduces what schizophrenia is and how it affects the person you are supporting. It outlines the phases of schizophrenia, the symptoms associated with the disorder, the possible causes of the disorder, and the myths, stereotypes and stigma associated with schizophrenia.

The word schizophrenia is used to describe a mental disorder that affects a person's thinking, feeling and behavior. It is the most common form of psychosis, where the person has some loss of contact with reality. In a person's lifetime, about 1 in 100 people will develop this disorder. In terms of age range, the disorder will usually start between a person's late teens to mid-30s. Although gender distribution is roughly the same, women are more likely than men to develop schizophrenia at a slightly older age.

Contrary to previous beliefs, the majority of people with schizophrenia lead fulfilling lives, with many learning to manage their disorder effectively, gain employment, have lasting relationships, and start a family. Today, many people with schizophrenia do not have to go into hospital.

It is important to remember that recovery from schizophrenia is possible. According to the United Kingdom Royal College of Psychiatrists, for every five people who have schizophrenia:

- One will get better within five years of their first obvious symptoms.

- Three will get better, but will have times when they get worse again.

- One will have troublesome symptoms for long periods of time.

With schizophrenia, recovery does not necessarily mean the same thing as recovery from a physical illness. Instead, the focus on recovery from schizophrenia is on the person learning to manage their disorder, cope with their symptoms, live well and lead a fulfilling life.

Experiencing schizophrenia

Each person will experience schizophrenia differently and may have a variety of symptoms. These experiences are so real to the person that they often do not realize they are experiencing schizophrenia. This affects how they think, feel and behave. A person may have periods of time when the symptoms are strong and interfere with day-to-day life. They may not realize that they are ill, or may not understand what is happening to them. This impaired awareness of their condition is a core feature of psychosis and varies depending on the severity of the person's illness and where they are in their recovery.

Although the type and severity of symptoms of schizophrenia vary from person to person, they may continue for weeks, months or even years. The symptoms may even disappear; however, the person remains at risk of the symptoms returning. A diagnosis involves assessing a person's symptoms and the course of their disorder.

Phases of schizophrenia

There are four phases of schizophrenia, but not every person will experience clear features of all four phases. Each person's experience will be different.

Phase 1: Prodromal phase

Many people will experience a "prodrome," which may last one to five years. A prodrome is the time interval from when the person displays some early unusual behavioral symptoms (or pre-psychotic symptoms) to the actual onset of the acute or fully developed symptoms that are characteristic of the disorder. Symptoms of the prodrome can include changes in the person's feelings or thoughts, and they may not be able to function in their usual way. Other people might not even notice the prodrome, although you may be aware that there are slight changes in the way the person feels, thinks and behaves.

During the prodrome phase, the person, you, family or friends may not understand what is happening, which may result in conflict or arguments. People may think that the person is going through a difficult stage in their life or displaying challenging behavior. This is understandable, as it is often difficult to recognize a prodrome from adolescent (youth) issues or behaviors associated with regular substance (alcohol and drug) use.

Phase 2: Acute phase

This is when the person experiences clear "positive" and "negative" symptoms of schizophrenia, such as hallucinations (false perceptions, such as hearing voices no one else can hear) and delusions (false beliefs), or when behavioral changes (such as aggressive behavior, poor personal hygiene and/or social withdrawal) become more obvious.

A detailed assessment of the person is required and treatment is usually started as soon as possible. Some people can be treated at home, while others may need intensive care in a hospital. During this phase, the person may not have any awareness of their disorder. Self-care for families and carers is extremely important at this time.

Phase 3: Recovery phase

During the recovery phase, the person's symptoms of schizophrenia begin to fade, although the process of recovery is different for each person. There may be periods of improvement mixed with periods of difficulties or setbacks. This is normal, as people rarely have a smooth transition back to health.

During the recovery phase, the person may experience depression and anxiety, have less energy and motivation, or withdraw from social interactions. Most people recover significantly (if not completely) from a first episode of schizophrenia.

Further information about recovery is provided in Chapter 6.

Phase 4: Relapse

The early course of schizophrenia is often unsettled, and many affected individuals will experience a return of acute symptoms of the disorder within five years (relapse). Relapse means that the person's mental condition has deteriorated to the extent that signs and symptoms associated with the acute phase of the disorder have returned. This is often caused by a variety of factors such as stress, ceasing medication and substance use. Sometimes, however, relapse may have no apparent cause.

Relapse is often a blow to the person's sense of hope and makes it hard for them to maintain employment, study or engage in social activities. During this phase, the person may need to return to hospital.

Preventing relapse is vital to the person's recovery. Detecting early warning signs of relapse, seeking help as soon as possible and sticking to the treatment plan can achieve this. Generally, the earlier the person gets help when showing early signs and symptoms of relapse, the better the outcome will be.

Sticking to a treatment plan involves taking medication as prescribed, maintaining a healthy lifestyle, engaging in stress management, getting support from friends, family and services, educating themselves and others about the disorder, and taking part in therapy where prescribed.

Unfortunately, even if the person sticks to the treatment plan, relapse is still possible, but the person will be in a better position to detect signs and symptoms earlier.

Several signs and symptoms, which may be obvious or unclear, suggest a relapse. The following section describes different groups of signs and symptoms that may occur.

Symptoms of schizophrenia

Schizophrenia can lead to changes in the person's mood, thinking and behavior. Four main types of symptoms occur in schizophrenia, especially in the "acute phase": positive, negative, cognitive and affective symptoms. These symptoms vary from person to person and may change over time. Moreover, not everyone experiences all of the symptoms; for example, carers sometimes say, "He can't have schizophrenia, because he has never heard voices."

Positive symptoms

Positive symptoms are called "positive" because they are viewed as "in addition" to what people normally experience. A person with positive symptoms frequently loses touch with reality. Common positive symptoms include hallucinations, delusions and thought and movement disorders.

- **Hallucinations** involve the person hearing, seeing, smelling, feeling or tasting things that no one else can hear, see, smell, feel or taste. The most common type of hallucination is where the person hears voices that no one else can hear.

- **Delusions** are false beliefs that are not shared by others in the person's community or culture. These false beliefs do not change and are not logical or true.

  - **Paranoid beliefs** are another form of delusion, where the person feels others are trying to harm them. Like other types of delusions, paranoid beliefs do not change and are not logical or true.

- **Thought disorders** are dysfunctional or unusual ways of thinking, resulting in abnormal ways of expressing spoken and written language. There are two forms (and many types) of thought disorder:

  - **Disorganized (confused) thinking**, where the person has difficulty organizing their thoughts or connecting them together in a logical way. Examples are "thought blocking," where the person stops talking abruptly in the middle of a sentence, and "looseness of association," where the person may switch frequently from one topic to another topic.

– **Disorganized speech**, where the person has difficulty with their speech and it may be difficult to understand what they are saying. Disorganized speech is often called "incoherence" or "word salad."

• **Disorganized or abnormal motor behavior**, where the person's body movements are affected. Most commonly, this appears like agitated body movements, where the person repeatedly carries out certain movements. Another much less common form of movement disorder is catatonia, where the person does not move or respond to others around them. (Note: In 2018, the World Health Organization recognized the syndrome of catatonia as a separate diagnostic grouping that can occur in association with several mental disorders, including schizophrenia.)

Negative symptoms

Negative symptoms are thoughts, feelings or behaviors normally present that are absent or diminished in a person with schizophrenia. These symptoms are more difficult to recognize and are sometimes mistaken for depression or other conditions. Examples of negative symptoms include diminished motivation, drive or interests, reduced experience of pleasure in everyday life, difficulty initiating and sustaining activities, limited displays of emotion or speaking in a monotonous voice, not talking very much or being vague, and limited interest in interacting with others.

Cognitive symptoms

Cognitive symptoms relate to the way the person thinks. Cognitive symptoms may be difficult to recognize as part of schizophrenia. Cognitive symptoms include impairments in thinking, such as difficulties with memory and concentration or paying attention, thinking more slowly, difficulty in understanding information and in using this information to make decisions, and impaired awareness of their disorder or its impact on others.

Affective symptoms

Affective symptoms relate to the person's mood. Affective symptoms include depressed mood (feeling low, not enjoying life, feeling worthless or hopeless), elevated mood (feeling high or overconfident) or irritability (feeling easily frustrated with others or aggressive). Affective symptoms may occur within one specific phase of schizophrenia.

Diagnosis of schizophrenia

Initially, it is uncommon for the person to be diagnosed with schizophrenia. Instead, the term "psychotic episode" or "psychosis" is used. It is only when the person has definite symptoms of schizophrenia (a particular form of psychotic disorder) for at least six months that a diagnosis of schizophrenia is made.

Causes of schizophrenia

There are many theories about why schizophrenia develops, but there is no definite cause. The most common theories implicate genetics, brain chemistry, use of some psychoactive drugs or substances and a combination of vulnerability and stress.

Genetics

People may have an increased risk of developing schizophrenia if they have close relatives who have already experienced the disorder. It is important to note that a family history of schizophrenia does not mean that other family members will definitely develop schizophrenia, but it is more likely if they are also exposed to other risk factors. The genetics of schizophrenia is an extremely complex issue, and at present there is limited understanding of how genetic factors increase the risk for schizophrenia.

In the general population, the risk of developing schizophrenia is approximately 1 percent. However, for children of people with schizophrenia, the lifetime risk of developing schizophrenia is 13 percent. Siblings (brothers and sisters) of people with schizophrenia have a lifetime risk of 9 percent of developing schizophrenia.

New research has hypothesized that a person's risk of developing schizophrenia is increased if they inherit a gene abnormality that reduces the number of connections (synapses) between neurons in the brain. This finding may help explain why people with schizophrenia have a reduced number of connections in their brains.

Brain chemistry

There is strong evidence that schizophrenia involves changes in how the brain's chemical messengers (neurotransmitters) normally work. Neurotransmitters are central to how communication occurs throughout the brain and the central nervous system. Of particular importance for schizophrenia is the neurotransmitter dopamine, which appears to be overactive in some parts of the brain and underactive in other parts of the brain. Other neurotransmitters may also be affected.

Dopamine is a neurotransmitter that is involved in mood, movement, learning and memory, decision-making and experiences of pleasure and pain. Most antipsychotic drugs are thought to be effective in treating the positive symptoms of schizophrenia by targeting an overactive dopamine system.

Psychoactive drugs or substances

These are substances that, when taken, affect the way the person thinks and feels. In some individuals, use of marijuana and some other "street" drugs may trigger a psychotic episode, which, in turn, may progress to schizophrenia.

Vulnerability and stress

A person's vulnerability (susceptibility) to schizophrenia may be due to their genetic predisposition, or because of harmful environmental influences on the brain. A history of birth complications, childhood trauma and head injuries during childhood have all been associated with vulnerability to schizophrenia.

Life stresses may trigger the onset of schizophrenia. Stressful situations include:

- Significant life events (for example, the death of a family member, moving to a new city or country, starting a new job or studies).

- Use of some psychoactive drugs or substances by vulnerable individuals.

- Stressful living conditions (for example, family conflict, family violence or financial problems).

In situations like these, it is thought that if people who are vulnerable to schizophrenia experience extreme and/or prolonged stress, they may develop schizophrenia.

The degree of vulnerability to schizophrenia varies from person to person. The amount of stress that may trigger schizophrenia is also different for each person.

The following diagram shows the relationship between a person who is vulnerable to schizophrenia and different types of stress (stressors).

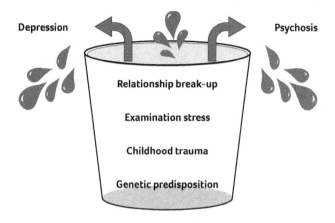

The bucket symbolizes a person's level of vulnerability and their capacity to deal with stress. When the bucket becomes filled with stressors, or when outside forces put pressure on the bucket, the bucket may overflow and psychiatric symptoms such as schizophrenia or depression may occur.

For example, a person with a low vulnerability (such as someone with *no* genetic predisposition) might be able to cope with a number of stressors (such as a relationship break-up and ongoing family conflict) without experiencing schizophrenia.

In contrast, a person with a high vulnerability (such as someone *with* a genetic predisposition) might only be able to cope with a small amount of stress (such as examination stress) before experiencing schizophrenia.

Myths, facts, stereotypes and stigma

Unfortunately, unhelpful myths and stereotypes about mental disorder and schizophrenia are still common in the community. Stigma or shame about mental disorder persists despite advances in modern medicine and community awareness programs promoted by mental health organizations. This is mostly due to people's ignorance of mental disorder, as many people are afraid of the unknown. Many people, including the family and friends of a person with schizophrenia, are afraid to discuss the person's disorder in front of others, while others are afraid to seek help.

Here are a number of common myths about mental illness and schizophrenia, all of which are false:

Myth: Bad parenting, passive fathers or domineering mothers cause schizophrenia.

Fact: There is no evidence that schizophrenia is caused by bad parenting, passive fathers or domineering mothers.

Myth: People with schizophrenia can never recover.

Fact: While there is no cure for schizophrenia, many people with the disorder can lead independent and fulfilling lives.

Myth: People with schizophrenia have developmental delay.

Fact: People with schizophrenia do not have developmental delay. This myth may have a basis in the nineteenth- and early twentieth-century practice of placing people with mental disorder and developmental delay in the same asylum. However, this practice was discontinued in most countries in the twentieth century.

Myth: People with schizophrenia have a low level of intelligence.

Fact: People with schizophrenia do not have a low level of intelligence. Their intelligence level varies, just like the rest of the population. Many famous people have schizophrenia; for example, John Nash, the mathematician who won the 1994 Nobel Prize in Economics and who inspired the film *A Beautiful Mind*.

Myth: People with schizophrenia are usually violent.

Fact: People with schizophrenia are not usually violent. In fact, they are more likely to be the victims of violence.

Myth: The risk of suicide in people with schizophrenia is no different to the general community.

Fact: People with schizophrenia have a higher risk of suicide than the general community. Approximately 10 percent (particularly young adult males) die by suicide.

Myth: Schizophrenia means split personality and there is no way to control it.

Fact: People with schizophrenia have only one personality.

Fortunately, the negativity surrounding mental disorder has been slowly diminishing over recent decades. This is mainly due to greater openness and discussion about mental disorder, improvements in people's understandings of mental disorder and better awareness of how common mental disorder is within the community. However, many people across all ages, cultures and nationalities believe in the myths and stereotypes about mental disorder and schizophrenia.

Chapter 5 provides further information about the stigma associated with schizophrenia and mental disorder and describes ways to challenge this stigma.

KEY POINTS TO REMEMBER

- Schizophrenia is a mental disorder that affects a person's thinking, emotion and behavior. It is the most common form of psychosis, where the person has some loss of contact with reality.

- The experience of schizophrenia can be different for each person. Common symptoms of schizophrenia include:

  - Hallucinations (false perceptions).

  - Delusions (false beliefs).

  - Paranoia (feeling persecuted).

  - Disorganized (confused) thoughts and speech.

  - Negative symptoms (disruptions to the person's normal emotions and behaviors).

  - Disorganized or abnormal motor (movement) behavior.

- There are four different "phases" of schizophrenia, but not every person will experience clear features of each phase.

- Many people with schizophrenia lead fulfilling lives. In today's mental health systems, many people with schizophrenia do not have to be admitted to hospital.

- There are no definite causes as to why people develop schizophrenia. However, people have an increased risk of developing schizophrenia if they have close relatives with the disorder.

- Unhelpful myths and stereotypes about mental disorder are common in the community. Myths and stereotypes can be challenged.

CHAPTER 3

Understanding Treatment

What does treatment involve?

Treatment of schizophrenia may involve a combination of medication and psychosocial treatments, such as stress management, family therapy, support groups, social and life skills therapies, psychological therapies, psychoeducation, mindfulness, the *Hearing Voices* approach and the *Open Dialogue* approach. These treatments/therapies/approaches will be described in more detail in this chapter. It is important the person understands the reason for treatment, the symptoms of the disorder, why a certain treatment method is used, how a treatment works and how long it will last.

If possible, try to learn about the different types of treatment available. It will help you provide support throughout the acute and recovery phases and encourage the person to stick to the treatment plan.

Treatment usually begins in the acute phase of the condition and may vary depending on the person's progress. Likewise, your level of involvement in the treatment will vary depending on the phase of the disorder. For instance, the person may experience hallucinations or delusions in the acute phase, where you may be required to provide constant support and care (however, this may also be the time when the person has impaired awareness of their disorder, where they are least able to recognize or accept the need for help and support). In the recovery phase, the person may need less care. You can discuss with the health professional what your level of involvement should be.

This chapter describes the importance of medication in treating schizophrenia and the side effects of taking medication. It also provides information on some psychosocial forms of treatment available that may be used in the person's treatment plan, or which you may find interesting.

Using medication

Medication is often necessary in the treatment of schizophrenia. It works best when combined with other forms of therapy. Medication may help to relieve symptoms such as hallucinations, delusions, anxiety, agitation, mood problems and social withdrawal. It is necessary to find the right type and dosage of medication, with the least side effects, to treat the symptoms. Please understand this takes time, as people respond differently to individual medications. Be patient and do not lose hope.

In collaboration with the person with schizophrenia, keep a list of the medications the person is taking, including the dosage and the time of day they should be taken, how long they are to be taken for, what symptoms they were meant to relieve and potential side effects. Again, in collaboration with the person, bring the list to meetings with the health professional to confirm what is on the person's medical file. Remember that medications work well for many people, but do not suit everyone. Similar to the use of medications to control high blood pressure or diabetes, medications for people with schizophrenia control the illness, but do not cure it.

There are four main types of medications used in the treatment of people with schizophrenia. Which types of medications are used will depend on the person's present symptoms, previous response to medications, and the prescriber's clinical judgement about what might work best in this situation.

The four main types of medications are:

- Medications to treat psychosis.

- Medications to treat side effects (for example, anticholinergics).

- Medications to treat mood disturbance (mood stabilizers and antidepressants).

- Medications to treat anxiety (anxiolytics).

The following information is provided as a guide and is not exhaustive. If you have any concerns about medications, please consult the health professional. Also, note that most medications have two names:

- The generic name, which is the chemical name of the drug (for example, olanzapine, risperidone or quetiapine).

- The brand or trade name given by the manufacturer (for example, in Australia, one brand name for olanzapine is Zyprexa, Risperdal for risperidone and Seroquel for quetiapine). Some medications have two or more brand names because different manufacturers produce them, and brand names for the same drug produced by the same company can vary across countries.

Antipsychotics

Antipsychotics are the main type of medication used to treat the positive and negative symptoms of schizophrenia, and they help many people return to a normal life. They help with anxiety and agitation, make the person feel less threatened, and reduce disorganized, aggressive and manic behaviors.

Although these medications may control the schizophrenia, they do not cure it. The person has to continue taking the medication to prevent symptoms returning. Even if the medication helps, the symptoms may return. This is much less likely to happen if the person continues taking medication. A small number of people, between 5 percent and 25 percent, do not respond to the usual antipsychotics and may need to try several medications and other therapies to gain control over their disorder.

There are two broad categories of antipsychotic medication: typical (first generation or older) and atypical (second generation or newer). Typical antipsychotics were released in the 1950s and 1960s, while atypical antipsychotics were released from the 1990s onwards.

Typical antipsychotics are effective but often have more side effects than atypical antipsychotics, especially if used in high doses. Most people are prescribed atypical antipsychotics, but some people may be prescribed typical antipsychotics because they respond better to this group of drugs.

Antipsychotic medications include:

- Atypical antipsychotics

    - These include olanzapine, risperidone, clozapine, quetiapine, amisulpride, aripiprazole, brexpiprazole, asenapine, ziprasidone, lurasidone and paliperidone.

    - Atypical antipsychotics are effective in the treatment of positive symptoms and may also help negative and cognitive symptoms (for example, social withdrawal, not speaking very much, difficulties in thinking or coming up with ideas, and decreased ability to initiate tasks).

- Typical antipsychotics

    - These include drugs such as chlorpromazine and haloperidol.

    - Typical antipsychotics are particularly effective in the treatment of positive symptoms (for example, hallucinations, delusions and disorganized speech or behavior).

Side effects

Antipsychotics have a wide range of side effects that may need to be monitored. Fortunately, most settle within the first few weeks of beginning treatment. A major problem with typical antipsychotics is that they produce neurological side effects such as tremor, slow movements, muscle spasm and restlessness. Some atypical antipsychotics produce major side effects such as weight gain and obesity, cardiovascular disease and metabolic problems like type 2 diabetes.

Together with the person with schizophrenia, it is important to monitor and tell the health professional about any changes or new symptoms the person experiences, as these may be side effects of the medication. Side effects may be grouped under three headings:

- General side effects.

- Movement disorders.

- Tardive dyskinesia.

GENERAL SIDE EFFECTS

- Sedation: feeling sleepy.

- Dry mouth: medication can reduce the amount of saliva secreted in the mouth. The person may experience dryness in the mouth, may not taste food properly or have cracked lips. Reduced saliva may also lead to trouble swallowing or speaking, and poor oral health and dental problems.

- Weight gain: this is linked to increased appetite and food intake, and decreased activity, but is mainly caused by changes in metabolism (the way the body uses food and converts it to energy or stores it as fat). As stated above, weight gain is particularly associated with atypical antipsychotics.

- Gastrointestinal problems, such as nausea (feeling sick), diarrhea or constipation associated with typical and atypical antipsychotics. However, these may also be affected by the person's diet, hydration and physical activity.

- Galactorrhea: excessive or inappropriate production of breast milk.

- Sexual dysfunction in males and females. For example, a drop in sexual desire in men and women, and ejaculation problems in men.

- Metabolic syndrome: this group of symptoms (weight gain and obesity, high blood sugar, high blood pressure and high cholesterol) puts people at risk of heart disease, stroke and diabetes, and, as stated above, is especially associated with some atypical antipsychotics. The risk is increased by dietary factors, such as drinking sugary, carbonated drinks and eating lots of fatty, sugary foods. Everyone, especially those with a family history of diabetes, should have their blood sugar tested while taking antipsychotic medications. Metabolic syndrome is thought to double or triple the risk of death from cardiovascular diseases.

MOVEMENT DISORDERS

These side effects are more common with typical antipsychotics, but are less common today because most people are prescribed atypical antipsychotics:

- Muscle spasm (dystonia).

- Tremor, slow movements (called Parkinson-like symptoms).

- Feeling restless or inability to sit still (akathisia).

TARDIVE DYSKINESIA

Tardive dyskinesia is a rare effect of antipsychotic medications that occurs in 5 percent of people, mainly those who take typical antipsychotics. It involves uncontrollable movements of facial muscles (for example, chewing or lip smacking). Tardive dyskinesia usually affects the face, but the limbs can also be involved. It does not usually appear until the person has been taking the medication for two or more years, and it may be irreversible. Studies have found that atypical antipsychotic medications have much lower rates of tardive dyskinesia than typical antipsychotic medications.

Blood tests

If the person is taking clozapine, blood tests are taken weekly initially. This is a precaution as clozapine can reduce the number of white blood cells (cells that help fight infection) when it is first taken. Blood tests are needed for as long as the person takes clozapine, but are done less frequently (monthly) after the first six months.

For how long should medication be taken?

Some people need to continue taking antipsychotic medication for a long period of time, perhaps the rest of their lives. Others are more fortunate and only need to continue taking the medication for one to two years after recovering from the acute phase of the disorder. In the early years, there is a high risk of relapse, and if people experience another acute phase, they may need to take antipsychotic medication for two to five years before considering ceasing antipsychotic treatment. People who have frequent acute episodes may need to take medication for the rest of their lives.

Medication that does not work

If symptoms have not improved after taking two or three antipsychotic medications, a thorough review is necessary. The health professional will need to check that the person has remembered to take the correct dose of medication as prescribed, and that other factors are not involved, such as a medical problem or the impact of regular substance use.

Psychological therapy may be provided to help the person cope with their symptoms, and a trial of clozapine may be offered. This medication produces good results when other treatments are not successful. However, as clozapine can produce some very serious side effects (as mentioned earlier), close monitoring is necessary to see if the person experiences any problems with this medication.

Psychosocial treatments

The term psychosocial relates to a person's psychological development in, and interaction with, their social environment. Even though medications are very important to treat psychosis, they are more effective when combined with certain psychosocial treatments. While there are many types of these treatments that you and the person may be able to use, there are different levels of scientific evidence to support their effectiveness. Nevertheless, some of the treatments with little or no evidence base may still be helpful for some individuals.

To find out more about psychosocial and other treatments, including how to access them, together with the person with schizophrenia, speak to the health professional. It is important that these types of treatment are discussed with them before commencement. These treatments are discussed in more detail below.

Stress management

Stress management involves being able to recognize stress and apply techniques to avoid or dispel the stress. After a person is able to identify when they are stressed, there are a number of ways for the person to deal with the stress, including:

- Anticipating stress: being prepared and developing ways to control what happens.

- Relaxation: calming one's body and mind.

- Realistic thinking: thinking about things realistically to overcome unhelpful thoughts.

- Reducing responsibilities and obligations: helps people cope when stress gets too much.

- Living well: regular exercise, eating and sleeping well, and goal-setting.

Stress management techniques for you and the person are explained further in Chapter 6.

Family interventions

There is no indication that families are in any way at fault in causing schizophrenia. Rather, they are just normal people trying to do their best in very difficult circumstances where it is not clear what they should do when problems arise. One effective way of assisting families to deal with problems in this situation is to use family interventions. These interventions seek to increase the quality of life of the person and the family, and help prevent the person relapsing to an acute form of schizophrenia. When people experience schizophrenia, their lives may change dramatically, as can the lives of their family and friends. Family interventions aim to improve the quality of life of the person and that of the family, and help everyone to function better together.

Family interventions involve improving communication patterns and conflict resolution between everyone, strengthening the relationship between the person and the family, and aiding the family's understanding of the illness and ability to cope. Families often claim that they need information, time to ask questions, practical and emotional support, and, sometimes, skills training. Most, if not all, families need and benefit from practical and emotional support and psychoeducation. However, not all need the more intensive forms of family interventions.

Multifamily group intervention

Multifamily group intervention (MFGI) is an evidence-based approach for treating people with schizophrenia and their families. It incorporates psychoeducation and behavioral family therapy and is delivered by mental health professionals to groups of five to eight families over a prolonged period (for example, over two years). MFGI increases social networking and support by assisting families to benefit from each other's experiences in solving problems, leading to a better course and outcomes of schizophrenia. MFGI has been shown to decrease the rate of relapse and re-hospitalization in the person with schizophrenia and improve the wellbeing of families.

Support groups

A support or self-help group is a group of people who have similar experiences and concerns who meet regularly to provide emotional help, advice, coping strategies and encouragement for one another. Some support groups meet online, via discussion boards or blogs. There are many types of mental health support groups for the person, carer and family, including some that are specific to schizophrenia. Support groups are led by a health professional, or are peer-led (that is, they are led by a person who has experienced the particular mental health disorder) or carer-led.

There is some evidence that mutual support groups may improve the person's, carer's and family's knowledge about the disorder, their coping and stress. A support group can help the person:

- Understand that other people have schizophrenia and have similar experiences.
- Develop new skills in relating to others.
- Openly discuss their emotions and situations.
- Learn from other people's experiences and share their own.
- Have a safe, non-judgemental place to discuss living with schizophrenia.
- Gain encouragement and support from others.
- Share experiences, which may help decrease stress and anxiety.
- Decrease social isolation.

Social and life skills training

Many people with schizophrenia have difficulty with everyday living tasks and social situations. They may have problems developing and maintaining relationships, and carrying out basic tasks, such as cooking, paying bills or shopping. Social and life skills training have been developed to help people overcome these types of difficulties. For example, the person may have to re-learn how to make a shopping list, go out shopping and interact with people as part of the process.

Psychological therapy

Psychological therapy is often referred to as talking therapy. It involves people talking about their problems, usually to mental health professionals. Several approaches are used in talking therapy to address a wide range of issues associated with the person's disorder, such as combating unhelpful thinking, dealing with the trauma of the disorder, or improving the person's medication taking. Talking therapy appears to be most effective when the person doing the talking and the person doing the listening have a good relationship with each other. Cognitive behavioral therapy, the talking therapy with the strongest evidence base, is summarized below.

Cognitive behavioral therapy

Cognitive behavioral therapy (CBT) aims to help the person change patterns of thinking or behavior that cause problems. Changing how the person thinks and behaves also changes how they feel. It is a structured approach, where the person agrees goals for treatment with a therapist and tries new ways of doing things. It helps the person to think more rationally and change unhelpful patterns of thinking. CBT is provided by a therapist with specialized training in the approach, and has a strong evidence base as an effective psychological therapy.

CBT may be helpful in:

- Reducing some symptoms of schizophrenia, such as auditory hallucinations (hearing voices).

- Reducing anger or depression.

- Improving medication taking.

- Reducing drug and alcohol use.

- Improving social and work skills.

- Enhancing ability to deal with stress.

- Increasing acceptance of the disorder.

Psychoeducation

Psychoeducation involves educating the person about their mental disorder to help empower them to make decisions about, and cope with, the disorder and treatment. Psychoeducation also involves educating the carer, family members and friends alongside the person.

According to research, people with a mental disorder who undertake psychoeducation are in a better position to cope with their disorder, and friends and family who undertake psychoeducation are in a better position to cope with the situation.

The goals of psychoeducation for schizophrenia can be described as learning about coping skills, problem-solving skills, signs of relapse, medicine and treatment, how to manage stress, and gaining a high level of knowledge about schizophrenia. This book is an example of a form of psychoeducation.

Mindfulness

The mindfulness approach is founded on Eastern meditation practices. It involves a person using meditation, breathing and yoga to concentrate on the present moment and helps the person be aware of their emotions, reactions and thoughts when dealing with everyday life. The approach is related to cognitive behavioral therapy in that it can help change a person's pattern of thinking and behavior. The approach has been used to treat depression, stress and anxiety.

Developing mindfulness skills may be helpful in alleviating the distress associated with schizophrenia rather than focusing solely on controlling the symptoms of schizophrenia, such as voices and paranoid thoughts.

Practicing mindfulness skills may help a person:

- Consciously bring awareness to the person's present circumstances (sometimes called the "here and now experience").

- Safely experience unpleasant thoughts and feelings.

- Become aware of what they are avoiding.

- Become more connected to themselves, to others and to the world around them.

- Become less judgemental.

- Increase self-awareness.

- Become less disturbed by and less reactive to unpleasant experiences.

- Learn the distinction between themselves and their thoughts.

- Have more direct contact with the world, instead of being preoccupied with their thoughts.

- Learn that everything changes, that thoughts and feelings come and go like the weather.

- Have more balance and less emotional volatility.

- Experience more calm and peacefulness.

There is some scientific evidence that mindfulness has a medium effect on reducing stress. This approach is not one of the more traditional methods of treatment for symptoms associated with schizophrenia. More information about mindfulness can be obtained from the website of the University of Oxford's Mindfulness Centre.[1]

The *Hearing Voices* approach

The *Hearing Voices* approach applies to people who experience auditory hallucinations, or hear voices. It is a way of coping with hearing voices without using traditional forms of treatment, such as antipsychotic medication.

Hearing Voices is based on providing the person with coping strategies to deal with the voices and normalize the experience. It does not aim to eliminate the voices, but to help people understand, accept and adapt to their reality while regaining some control or power over their lives.

The approach involves the person attending a *Hearing Voices* support group with other voice hearers to share their experiences and have the opportunity to talk freely. The groups are peer-led by people who have experience hearing voices and have learned to cope with them.

Hearing Voices is based on the research of Marius Romme and Sandra Escher in the 1980s (Corstens *et al.* 2014; Romme and Escher 1989). They identified key factors in determining which people can cope well with hearing voices compared with people who feel distress when hearing voices. These include:

- Being able to set limits with the voices.

- Listening selectively to voices.

- Communicating more often with the voices.

- Being able to explain and make sense of the voices.

- Being more likely to discuss their voices with others.

- Having more social and supportive connections with other people.

- Having higher self-esteem.

The *Hearing Voices* approach is not one of the more traditional methods of

---

1   www.oxfordmindfulness.org

treatment for people who hear voices, and is not freely available everywhere. For more information about this approach, go to the Intervoice website.[2]

The *Open Dialogue* approach

The *Open Dialogue* approach was developed in Finland as an alternative to the traditional mental health system's approach to treating people diagnosed with psychoses such as schizophrenia.

Open Dialogue involves regular treatment meetings with the person, the family and social network, and mental health workers. Decisions about the person's treatment are made at treatment meetings only, and include the person. At present, research is being undertaken to further evaluate and test the approach.

The *Open Dialogue* approach is not one of the more traditional methods of treatment for schizophrenia, and is not freely available everywhere.[3]

KEY POINTS TO REMEMBER ────────────────────

- Treatment of schizophrenia involves a combination of medication and psychosocial treatment.

- It is important for the person and the carer to understand all aspects of the treatment plan before it commences. Do not hesitate to enquire about the treatment plan.

- Medications work well for many people. They control the disorder, but they do not cure it. Antipsychotic medication can have a number of side effects. It is important to inform the health professional about any changes or new symptoms the person experiences.

- It is helpful to bring a list of the types of medicine the person is taking to meetings with the health professional. The length of time a person needs to take medication varies.

- Further information about, and how to access, psychosocial forms of treatment can be sought from the person's health professional. It is helpful to consult the health professional before commencing any psychosocial treatment.

---

2   www.intervoiceonline.org

3   For more information about this approach go to www.madinamerica.com/tag/open-dialogue; https://opendialogue.org.au; http://opendialogueapproach.co.uk; http://willhall.net/opendialogue; www.dialogicpractice.net

Introducing Problem-Solving

Problem-solving for carers

People experience problems every day. Most of the time these problems are small, like losing keys, being late or getting stuck in traffic. Some of these daily problems may be more significant, like having an argument with a friend or family member, not having enough money to pay for things, or failing to complete some work. These problems may appear small, but they can cause significant stress if they continue to grow over time. It is best if we can resolve our problems as early as possible.

People may also experience big problems, such as the death of a friend or family member, moving to another country, becoming ill or losing a job. Major problems may create additional smaller problems that may make the original problem worse. For example, when experiencing a major problem, a person who has schizophrenia may find it difficult to carry out daily tasks, such as shopping or cleaning up. Both types of problem, big and small, may lead to additional stress.

Problem-solving means thinking about how to come up with a solution to a problem. There are several problem-solving methods, but they all tend to be similar. Once you have learnt and practiced a method several times, it becomes a valuable skill that can be used over and over again to help you through everyday life.

As a carer of a person who has schizophrenia, you may find yourself experiencing a lot of new challenges or problems as a result of the person's disorder. It is helpful if you can solve these problems quickly and effectively, so you can lessen your stress and get on with everyday life.

Problem-solving self-assessment test

This book uses the problem-solving approach from the book *Solving Life's Problems,*[1] written by Arthur Nezu, Christine Maguth Nezu and

---

1   With the permission of the Springer Publishing Company, New York.

Thomas D'Zurilla. Before learning this approach, it is important to evaluate your present problem-solving ability, attitudes and beliefs.

One way to work out your problem-solving ability is to use a self-assessment test. This helps you identify your strengths and limitations, while highlighting the areas where you need the most practice.

Before you begin the test, think of something important in your life that bothers you a lot, but you do not know how to make it better or make it stop. This could be something about yourself (such as your appearance, health or behavior), your interactions with other people (such as family, friends, teachers or employer), or your personal property (such as your house, car or money). When you think of something, write it down below.

Once you have done this, you are ready to take the test. Read carefully through each statement in Table 4.1 and choose which of the numbers, from 1 to 5 in the 5-point scale, best describes how much that statement is true of you when you are faced with a problem. Enter this number in the corresponding blank space in the third column. The test is not about judging if you are a good or bad person, or if you are good at things—it is about identifying your strengths and weaknesses so you can become a more effective problem solver. Try not to feel pressured.

Table 4.1 Problem-solving self-assessment test

Answer each statement using the scale 1–5:
1 = Not at all true of me   2 = Somewhat true of me   3 = Moderately true of me
4 = True of me   5 = Very true of me

No.	How much is this statement true of you?	Your response 1–5
1	I feel very afraid when I have an important decision to solve.	
2	When making decisions, I think carefully about my many options.	
3	I get nervous and unsure of myself when I have to make an important decision.	
4	When my first efforts to solve a problem fail, I give up quickly, because finding a solution is too difficult.	
5	Sometimes even difficult problems have a way of moving my life forward in positive ways.	
6	If I avoid problems, they will generally take care of themselves.	
7	When I am unsuccessful at solving a problem, I get very frustrated.	
8	If I work at it, I can learn to solve difficult problems effectively.	
9	When faced with a problem, before deciding what to do, I carefully try to understand why it is a problem by sorting it out, breaking it down and defining it.	

cont.

No.	How much is this statement true of you?	Your response 1–5
10	I try to do anything I can to avoid problems in my life.	
11	Difficult problems make me very emotional.	
12	When I have a decision to make, I take the time to try to predict the helpful and unhelpful consequences of each possible option before I act.	
13	When I am trying to solve a problem, I often rely on instinct with the first good idea that comes to my mind.	
14	When I am upset, I just want to run away and be left alone.	
15	I can make important decisions on my own.	
16	I frequently react before I have all of the facts about a problem.	
17	After coming up with an idea of how to solve a problem, I work out a plan to carry it out successfully.	
18	I am very creative about coming up with ideas when solving problems.	
19	I spend more time worrying about problems than actually solving them.	
20	My goal for solving problems is to stop unhelpful feelings as quickly as I can.	
21	I try to avoid any trouble with others to keep problems to a minimum.	
22	When someone upsets me or hurts my feelings, I always react the same way.	
23	When I am trying to figure out a problem, it helps me to stick to the facts of the situation.	
24	In my opinion, being systematic and logical with personal problems seems too cold or "business-like."	
25	I understand that emotions, even bad ones, can actually be helpful to my efforts at problem-solving.	

Before you score yourself, let's look at the major problem-solving dimensions that the test evaluates. Based on many years of clinical research, Nezu, Nezu and D'Zurilla have come up with five dimensions of real-life problem-solving. The five dimensions describe the strengths and weaknesses that people have towards problem-solving. Two of the dimensions are about "problem orientation," which refers to the manner in which people think and feel about problems in general, as well as their ability to cope successfully with them. The remaining three dimensions are about "problem-solving style," which refers to the way in which people react or respond to stressful problems.

Problem orientation

1. Positive problem orientation

A positive problem orientation is associated with "successful problem-solving." A person with a positive problem orientation has the tendency to:

- View a problem as a challenge rather than a threat.

- Be realistically optimistic that problems are solvable.

- Have the self-confidence to believe in their ability to be a successful problem solver.

- Understand that solving difficult problems takes persistence and effort.

- Commit to solving the problem rather than avoiding it.

2. Unhelpful problem orientation

An unhelpful problem orientation is associated with "unsuccessful problem-solving." A person with an unhelpful problem orientation has the tendency to:

- View the problem as a major threat to their wellbeing.

- Doubt their personal ability to solve a problem.

- Generally become frustrated, upset and emotionally distressed when confronted with problems.

Problem-solving styles

3. Rational problem-solving style

Rational problem-solving is a successful problem-solving style that refers to solving problems in a logical, systematic and deliberate way, or using a "scientific method" to solve problems in a careful and reasoned way. A person who solves problems rationally may gather facts about a problem, list alternative solutions and outcomes, come up with goals and develop action plans.

4. Impulsivity/carelessness style

Impulsivity/carelessness style is an unsuccessful problem-solving style in which a person attempts to solve a problem in a careless and hurried manner, or where the problem is not dealt with completely, or the range of options available are not used. For example, a person who displays this problem-solving style tends to consider only a few solutions to a problem, impulsively uses the first idea that comes to mind, and overlooks other options available and the overall outcome.

5. Avoidance style

Avoidance style is an unsuccessful problem-solving style. People with avoidance style tend to put off or delay attempts to solve problems. They may deny any existence of problems, depend on others to solve their problems and be passive when faced with solving problems.

Scoring your answers

Let's look at how you scored on your problem-solving self-assessment test. After learning about the five dimensions of problem-solving, you may have noticed how the test was designed to evaluate which problem-solving style and attitudes you use.

To score your answers and see your problem-solving strengths and weaknesses, use the calculations in Table 4.2 for each dimension and write your total scores in the "total score" column.

Table 4.2 Calculating your problem-solving strengths and weaknesses

Dimension	How to calculate score	Total score
Positive problem orientation	Add the scores for statement numbers 5, 8, 15, 23 and 25	
Rational problem-solving style	Add the scores for statement numbers 2, 9, 12, 17 and 18	
Unhelpful problem orientation	Add the scores for statement numbers 1, 3, 7, 11 and 16	
Impulsivity/carelessness style	Add the scores for statement numbers 4, 13, 20, 22 and 24	
Avoidance style	Add the scores for statement numbers 6, 10, 14, 19 and 21	

Your problem-solving strengths

Take your score for positive problem orientation and compare it using the description below:

- A score below 12 shows it may be beneficial if you receive education, training and practice to develop your problem-solving skills and improve your resistance to the stress of daily problems.

- A score between 12 and 18 shows you have some strengths, but may benefit from improving your rational problem-solving style, positive problem orientation or both.

- A score of 18 to 25 shows you already have a positive attitude and/or strong rational problem-solving skills.

Take your score for rational problem-solving style and compare it using the same description above.

Your problem-solving weaknesses

Take your score for unhelpful problem orientation:

- A score of 12 or higher shows you may have a tendency to think about problems incorrectly and have difficulty managing your emotions when you are under stress. The higher your score, the more unhelpful your problem-solving attitude is. However, by reading appropriate chapters in this book and completing accompanying problem-solving exercises, it is possible for you to learn how to change your unhelpful problem orientation.

Take your score for impulsivity/carelessness style:

- A score of 12 or higher shows you may have the tendency to make decisions before thinking about them and may often make decisions that are not in your best interest. However, it is possible for you to learn how to stop and think before acting.

Take your score for avoidance style:

- A score of 12 or higher shows you tend to avoid problems. This seriously affects how you are able to cope with problems. However, it is possible for you to learn to reduce any fears and anxieties you have when you are faced with a problem.

How did you score? Were you happy with the results? Were you surprised with the findings?

Don't be disappointed if your problem-solving skills are not quite as good as what you would like. Virtually everybody would struggle under similar circumstances. Special problem-solving strategies are needed that have been shown to be beneficial to carers in your situation.

ADAPT 5-step method to effective problem-solving

Now that you have gained a better understanding of your problem-solving strengths and weaknesses, and what you need to improve, let's look at the ADAPT method of effective problem-solving used in the book *Solving Life's Problems*. You will use this method in the activities throughout this book. The ADAPT acronym refers to the idea that through problem-solving a person can adapt or adjust more successfully to life's stresses and strains.

This method can help a person become better at problem-solving and coping with life's stresses. As far as possible, it is a good approach to involve the person with schizophrenia in this problem-solving process.

The five steps to effective problem-solving are as follows:

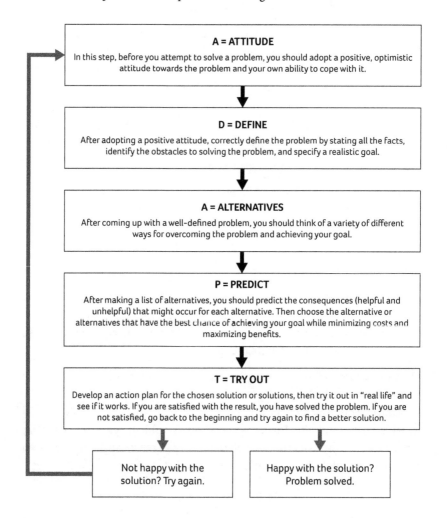

A = ATTITUDE

In this step, before you attempt to solve a problem, you should adopt a positive, optimistic attitude towards the problem and your own ability to cope with it.

D = DEFINE

After adopting a positive attitude, correctly define the problem by stating all the facts, identify the obstacles to solving the problem, and specify a realistic goal.

A = ALTERNATIVES

After coming up with a well-defined problem, you should think of a variety of different ways for overcoming the problem and achieving your goal.

P = PREDICT

After making a list of alternatives, you should predict the consequences (helpful and unhelpful) that might occur for each alternative. Then choose the alternative or alternatives that have the best chance of achieving your goal while minimizing costs and maximizing benefits.

T = TRY OUT

Develop an action plan for the chosen solution or solutions, then try it out in "real life" and see if it works. If you are satisfied with the result, you have solved the problem. If you are not satisfied, go back to the beginning and try again to find a better solution.

Not happy with the solution? Try again.

Happy with the solution? Problem solved.

Features of the ADAPT method

When using the ADAPT method of problem-solving:

- Make sure that you identify a problem or goal that you can work towards, rather than focusing on making someone else change their behavior. As far as possible, involve the person with schizophrenia in this problem-solving process.

- Avoid mixing problems: focus on one problem at a time.

- Be specific: ensure the problem is explained clearly.

- Brainstorm sufficient alternatives: otherwise you may end up not choosing the best option.

When you practice using the ADAPT method through this book, you may notice that your problem-solving ability improves. You can also apply the method to problems of your own that are not related to your experience as a carer.

Problem-solving is a life skill. Once you have learnt the ADAPT method, you can use it again and again. The more you practice effective problem-solving, the better you will be at solving life's problems and minimizing stress.

KEY POINTS TO REMEMBER ————————————————

As a carer, you may find that you experience a lot of new challenges or problems because of the person's disorder. By identifying your strengths and weaknesses, you will become a more effective problem solver.

A person with a positive problem orientation tends to:

- View a problem as a challenge rather than a threat.

- Be realistically optimistic that problems are solvable.

- Have the self-confidence to believe in their ability.

- Understand that problem-solving takes persistence and effort.

- Commit to solving the problem rather than avoiding it.

When using the ADAPT 5-step method of problem-solving, remember to:

- Identify a problem or goal that you can work towards, rather than focusing on changing someone's behavior.

- Concentrate on one problem at a time.

- Be specific—ensure the problem is explained clearly.

- Consider a range of suitable options.

Problem-solving is a life skill. The more you practice effective problem-solving, the better you will be at solving life's problems and minimizing stress.

CHAPTER 5

Looking After Yourself

Being a carer

Supporting someone close to you with schizophrenia can be difficult and demanding, yet it can be a rewarding experience. It often has a great impact on your overall wellbeing. You may need to make sacrifices; for instance, you may have less time to spend with family and friends, at work or social outings, or on yourself. It is important to have realistic expectations, as you will encounter many challenges in your new role, as well as having to deal with existing ones.

As a carer, you may feel underappreciated, overworked, stressed and anxious. This is not meant to intimidate or put you off being a carer, but to help you prepare for what lies ahead. It is important to look after your wellbeing, so you have the full opportunity to make your support role a rewarding experience. Once you overcome the initial challenges of your role, you should begin to find joy and satisfaction in what you are doing.

If you are used to being self-reliant, you may have to learn to ask for and accept help from other people. Being a carer is often a role that cannot be done alone—having someone to share the role of carer is the best type of support you can get. Various types of help are available.

This chapter provides you with information on how to look after yourself. It discusses the range of emotions that carers feel, suggests ways you can improve your wellbeing, encourages you to review your coping skills, describes how friends and family are affected by the disorder, and provides you with ways to challenge the stigma associated with schizophrenia.

Carers' emotions

As a carer, you may experience a range of conflicting emotions, including disbelief, frustration, shame and love. It is normal to feel these emotions throughout each phase of your support role. It is important to know that none of these feelings is right or wrong. It is also important to understand that other family members and close friends of the person will also feel these emotions. In addition, family members may experience conflicting emotions, which can create tension between them.

Some common emotions you, family members and friends may feel include the following.

Guilt

> I didn't know he was ill. If only I'd picked it up earlier. I thought it was just adolescence...

You may feel responsible for not seeking help earlier or blame yourself for the disorder. You may feel guilty about not wanting to be a carer or feel you are not doing enough to help.

Disbelief

> She's always acting up. I don't believe she's really ill. Mom just lets her get away with things.

At times you may disbelieve the person you are supporting is unwell because of their good or poor behavior.

Shame

> What will the neighbors think? I've had to ring the police and ambulance...

You may worry about what others think, or feel embarrassed. You may not tell many people what has happened.

Frustration

> She doesn't even seem to appreciate what I'm doing for her, nor does anyone else...

You may get frustrated or angry with them, or frustrated at being a carer. You may feel underappreciated or taken for granted by others.

Depression

I just feel so low. I can't do anything to help. I wish I could make a difference.

You may feel depressed at, what you feel is, the hopelessness of your situation.

Anxiety

I'm so worried when I leave him alone or when he goes out with friends. Will I ever feel okay about leaving him by himself?

You may feel anxious about what might happen when you are not around and what might happen in the future for the person.

Grief and loss

He stopped going to work. He loved that job. I don't know if he'll go back...

You may grieve for the loss of the person you knew before the onset of the disorder, and their loss of hopes and dreams. You may miss the life you had beforehand.

Love

I cherish the times I spend with her, they're not always good times, but I love her none the less...

Your love for the person may deepen or it may weaken, and sometimes it may be a mixture of the two.

These are just a few examples of the emotions you may be feeling. Remember, what you are feeling is normal and part of the experience of being a carer. You may find that these feelings and your motivation change over time.

ACTIVITY: Review and reflect

What type of emotions are you feeling as a carer?

_____

_____

_____

Talking to other people may help you overcome some emotions. Keeping them to yourself may make things worse. Try not to feel afraid or ashamed to talk to someone about how you feel. Every carer experiences similar emotions to what you are feeling. If you cannot talk to family or friends, there are support services available that welcome your call.

What emotions as a carer have you talked to others about (or would like to talk to others about)?

_____

_____

_____

Your wellbeing

To help you deal with your emotions and cope better, it is important to look after your own wellbeing. You need to look after yourself before you look after the needs of others, as it is difficult to help someone when you need help. Your first response may be: "I don't have the time to look after myself, nor the energy." This is understandable, but improving your wellbeing involves taking time out for yourself and your needs.

Here are some ways to improve your overall wellbeing.

Support

It is vital you receive as much support as possible from those around you, especially from family and friends. Is there someone who can share the role with you, even for a short time, on a regular basis? Having someone to share your experiences, or laugh or cry with, can give you comfort and strength and help reduce any feelings of isolation. This may be through telephone calls, emails, social outings or something as simple as getting help with household chores.

You can seek help from carer and mental health support services and support groups. There are services that offer counseling, provide information or can put you in contact with other carers. Simply talking with other people who are experiencing what you are will be extremely beneficial. There are support groups specifically for carers of people with mental health and schizophrenia; they may be face-to-face groups or accessible online. Each will have a different style, so it is important to find the one that suits you. Don't feel put off if you have a bad experience with one.

Managing stress

Learning how to manage your stress will help your overall wellbeing. Carers may experience more stress when they first take on the role, as they will have a new set of responsibilities, worries and tasks associated with supporting the person.

You can feel stressed at any time. The symptoms of stress—like tension, worry, anxiety or sleeplessness—may come and go, or they may continue for a long period. This can impact on your overall wellbeing.

There are ways to manage stress that involve future planning for when stressful times will occur. This planning involves identifying stress triggers and learning response techniques that will help lessen the stress or avoid the stress completely. Refer to the section on stress management in Chapter 6 for more information.

Exercise

Regular exercise improves your health and fitness and can benefit your mental and emotional wellbeing. It does not have to mean a trip to the gym; it can be as simple as a walk to the shops or doing some gardening. Try incorporating as much exercise in your day as possible, particularly outdoor exercise. Exercising with other people can encourage you to commit to exercising regularly.

Taking breaks

No one can be a carer every minute of every day. It is important to recognize your limits, have a break and do something you enjoy, such as having a day to yourself or taking a holiday. This will give you an opportunity for self-renewal. Is there a family member or friend who could take your place for a day? Is the person you are supporting well enough to look after themselves for a day? Is there respite care (short-term care of the person) you could access? For further information on respite care, ask a health professional or mental health support services.

Rest and relaxation

Rest and relaxation can help ease stress and lift your mood. This does not have to mean yoga, meditation or listening to pleasant music, although all of these pursuits are worthwhile. It may involve watching a film, reading a book or magazine, shopping, going out for dinner, doing odd jobs around the house, having a bath or seeing friends. Rest and relaxation involve doing something you enjoy.

Even doing something straightforward, like spending 15 minutes alone to read a newspaper or magazine, can make a difference. It can also involve avoiding extra pressures or unnecessary tasks, such as putting off chores for one day, ordering a takeaway meal, not bringing work home or getting others to help you tidy up.

Finding joy

Throughout your role, it is easy to become overwhelmed with the responsibilities and your emotions. To help you gain a positive experience of your support role, it is helpful to reflect on what you are doing. Try to find joy and satisfaction. You should feel good about small achievements. For example, the person you are supporting may begin to take their medication regularly without you prompting them, making you feel more trusting of them and pleased with the progress they have made, however small it may seem.

Think of the positive aspects of being a carer. For example, you may have a closer relationship with the person, knowing that you are the only one who can provide the best care for them. You may enjoy seeing them make progress and comforting them when they have setbacks, or being able to keep the person from going into hospital.

Finding happiness in your role will help you overcome the difficulties that you will experience.

Health

Maintaining a healthy lifestyle is important for all ages. Consider having regular health checks and seek medical assistance when you are ill. Putting off getting medical help or not taking the time to let your body rest and recuperate only makes matters worse. Most people's first medical contact person is their GP or family doctor. Do you have a GP who you respect and with whom you are comfortable discussing personal matters? Is your GP close by? Can you get appointments easily? For very minor ailments, a pharmacist or chemist may be able to help in some situations.

Obvious ways to reduce health risks include cutting back on cigarette smoking and excessive alcohol consumption, and on the use of non-prescribed medication, such as sedatives or stimulants.

Diet and nutrition

Consider what you are eating. Are you eating healthy meals? This is something you can get help with in various ways, through your GP, pharmacist or chemist, or online. Having a good diet and preparing regular meals may be difficult when you don't have much time, but it will help maintain your energy levels and physical and mental wellbeing.

A good diet involves eating three regular meals throughout the day and eating fresh vegetables, wholegrain or high-fiber foods, fruit and lean meats. It involves decreasing the amount of processed food you eat ("junk food" like burgers, chips, sweets [lollies], kebabs, pizza and fizzy drinks).

Sometimes you may not have the time to prepare fresh meals in your role. Takeaways are fine, as long as you don't eat them too often and choose healthy options. Other simple things you can change are decreasing the amount of sugar you have in hot drinks, swapping fizzy drinks for water and having a health snack—instead of reaching for a biscuit or a packet of chips, have a yoghurt, fruit or nuts. Small changes to your diet can go a long way towards maintaining good health.

Sleep

It is important to get adequate sleep to enable you to function properly every day. Sufficient sleep helps your alertness, memory, problem-solving and overall health, and reduces the risk of accidents. It is ideal to have seven to nine hours of sleep a night. In reality, not everyone gets this amount of sleep, especially if you are supporting someone and are awake at night worrying or feeling anxious. However, there are ways to improve your sleep. Helpful tips include:

- Getting up and writing down your thoughts and worries.

- Getting up and using distraction for a short while (for example, reading a book).

- Using relaxation tools specifically for sleep, such as sleep meditation, mobile phone/cell phone applications or relaxation CDs.

- Avoiding caffeinated and sugary drinks in the late afternoon and evening. This includes tea, coffee, cola and energy or soft drinks, although alternatives such as decaffeinated drinks may be consumed after lunch.

- Having a bedtime snack, like warm milk or toast.

- Making sure you are comfortable in your bed and warm enough.

- Having some quiet time to relax before going to sleep.

- Going to sleep and waking at the same times every day.

Planning

Planning ahead may help make things more manageable. Remember to include the person in the planning process. A daily routine can help structure the day. Include things such as meal breaks, activities and time for yourself. As mentioned before, planning for when stressful times occur will be very beneficial to you.

In addition, it is a good idea to make a plan of what to do in an emergency or a crisis. This may involve having a list of important telephone numbers on hand and knowing the best route to the mental health service. You may need to find a family member, friend or neighbor who can step in when you are unwell or while you are away.

ACTIVITY: Review and reflect

In what ways, if at all, do you look after your overall wellbeing?

_____

_____

_____

In what ways could you improve your overall wellbeing further?

_____

_____

_____

Your coping skills

Coping is a process where a person may be required to manage difficult circumstances, solve a problem, or overcome, reduce or tolerate stress or conflict. There are several coping mechanisms to help you in your role as a carer. A coping mechanism is basically a tool people use to deal with, offset or overcome problems or challenges. A coping mechanism will not necessarily fix or eliminate the underlying problem or condition, but it will help relieve the distress associated with it.

An example of a coping mechanism is seen in a teenager who, on hearing her parents arguing, retreats to her bedroom and telephones a friend. She is not addressing or overcoming the problem of her parents arguing, but is dealing with the situation in her own way. By distracting herself, she is minimizing the amount of stress she experiences. This may be viewed as a "helpful" coping mechanism. An "unhelpful" coping mechanism would be if she were to drink alcohol every time her parents argued. Every carer uses different helpful and unhelpful coping mechanisms.

Helpful coping mechanisms

- Getting support from services, friends or family.

- Exercising and relaxing.

- Spending time with family or friends.

- Treating yourself to something special, like going to the movies or cinema.

Unhelpful coping mechanisms

- Drinking alcohol, smoking cigarettes or using non-prescribed medication.

- Working harder.

- Withdrawing from social activities, family or friends.

- Sleeping less.

- Becoming moody.

- Engaging in self-harm behaviors.

ACTIVITY: Review and reflect

What coping mechanisms do you use?

_____

_____

_____

Do you see them as helpful or unhelpful coping mechanisms?

_____

_____

_____

Guidelines for coping

Here are some broad guidelines to help you cope better with the role you have taken on:

- Understand how you feel: recognize your emotions and understand they are normal and neither right nor wrong.

- Understand the disorder: educate yourself on the features of schizophrenia, treatment options, medications and their side effects.

- Understand the mental health system: familiarize yourself with how things happen at the mental health service, the roles of health professionals you come into contact with, your rights as a carer, and other services available to you.

- Come to terms with the fact that the person has the disorder: accept that you have no control over the disorder, you are not to blame, it takes time for the person to recover, and it is normal to feel the loss of what the person was like and aspired to be before the disorder.

- Adopt a positive outlook: give frequent praise to help both of you feel better, give yourself credit for the role you have undertaken, and reward yourself even when a small achievement has been made.

- Set realistic expectations: be realistic about what both of you can and cannot achieve, tackle difficult tasks one step at a time, learn to accept help from others, and seek support when things get too much for you to cope with.

- Look after yourself.

- Release unhelpful emotions safely; allow yourself to cry when feeling sad.

Older carers

Older carers may have a son, daughter, friend, partner or spouse with schizophrenia. At the same time, they may also be supporting older parents or have other family responsibilities such as grandchildren. All of this adds to their pressure of caring. Older carers need more breaks away from their support role, due to the likelihood of age-related health problems. This means having more periods of rest and relaxation on a daily basis, and taking breaks from their support role of not just a few hours, but a day or longer.

Older carers have persistent worries compared to other carers. These include:

- What happens when I am unfit to look after the person?

- What happens when I am no longer around?

- Who will look after them?

- What will happen to them?

- Who will pay to look after the person when I cannot?

- Who will look after my older parents or my grandchildren?

These constant worries cause a great deal of stress and anxiety that affect overall health and wellbeing.

If you are an older carer, consider trying to get as much support as possible from carer support services and mental health services. They may be able to provide respite care or help you get financial assistance to help you in your role (if financial assistance for carers is available in your country).

You can discuss all of your concerns, such as those above, with someone from a support service, the health professional and the person you are supporting. Together they can help you develop a plan for what will happen in emergencies and in the future.

As part of your planning, you may have to consider confronting issues, such as a will and guardianship of the person. You may not like to think about writing a will, but some things may not happen the way you would like them to if you die without a will.

Hopefully, making a plan will also help you feel more reassured about what will happen in the future. Carer support services may also be able to offer you counseling to help you deal with your worries and learn strategies to cope better.

Like other carers, you will need to develop a support network of friends, family and professionals who can help you in your day-to-day support role. Most importantly, you need to look after your health and wellbeing too and encourage the person to take responsibility for the management of their disorder.

Family and friends

Family and friends play an important role in helping their relative or friend recover from schizophrenia. When a person is recovering from schizophrenia, family and friends can provide love, stability, respect, understanding and reassurance, as well as help with practical issues.

Family and friends may experience frustration, disappointment, disbelief, anger or confusion when coming to terms with the fact that their loved one is unwell. Grief may be involved, as they may feel the loss of their loved one's former personality and achievements.

As a carer, it may be extremely helpful to involve this group in your support role. They may be able to help you, as well as the person with schizophrenia. Mental disorder affects all of the family. As discussed in Chapter 3, family therapies are available to help everyone involved find the best way to support the person, deal with problems that arise from living with someone with schizophrenia, help them to look after themselves emotionally and equip them with the skills to work collaboratively with health professionals.

Common experiences of families and friends

Jordan and Jessica don't get on as well as they used to since Jessica became ill. Jordan has a hard time coping with the changes in his sister and how everyone treats her differently. He feels that his mom, who is the main carer for Jessica, hardly has any time for him. Everything revolves around his sister. He can see that his parents are stressed and tense because they are afraid to upset Jessica or see her get worse. Jordan's older brother Brian avoids Jessica altogether. Brian is ashamed that Jessica has a mental disorder and is worried what people at his work might say.

Sometimes Jordan can see that Jessica is not well and needs help but other times he thinks she is just trying to get attention. He doesn't know how to act around her or whether she will be in a good mood or a low mood. They used to do so many things together, like go to the movies and see friends at the pub. He really misses the old Jessica.

Family and friends often go through similar experiences when a relative or friend has schizophrenia. It may be helpful to understand this to confirm what has happened and to prepare for what may happen next.

Family and friends may experience some of the following throughout the person's disorder:

- Initially, they may be in crisis as they become aware that something serious is happening to the person. They may feel anxious, worried and frightened.

- As it becomes clear that something is not quite right, they may start to seek help. It is also a time when they may be adjusting to the fact that the person is unwell and cannot be left to recover alone.

- When they seek help, they may not realize the seriousness of the situation. They may be overwhelmed as they watch the person being admitted to hospital or a clinic, especially if emergency services are called to help the person get admitted.

- As they find help, they may have lots of questions and worries, such as:

  - What is happening?

  - What is schizophrenia?

  - What causes it?

  - Will this happen again?

  - How is it treated?

  - Should we have got help earlier?

  - Are we to blame?

  - What can we do to help?

  - What should we tell other people?

  - Will our loved one understand why help is needed?

- They may have mixed emotions and reactions during this time. All of these are normal and understandable considering what is happening.

- As the person begins to show signs of recovery, they may experience great relief. They may also have more understanding of the disorder and start to feel hopeful about the future.

- As the recovery progresses, they may have many questions or concerns as the person begins to re-engage with everyone. They may find themselves watching them for signs of relapse or strange behavior. They may feel protective and anxious, wanting them to recover as quickly as possible and yet not wanting them to do anything that may lead to a relapse. They may find it difficult to allow the person to be independent as they try to care for them all of the time.

- If difficulties or setbacks occur in the recovery process, they may feel disheartened and frustrated with them.

- As recovery continues, there may be a gradual change in everyone involved. They may feel reassured that recovery is occurring and that things may return to normal. They may be able to speak with the person about schizophrenia, what it has been like for everyone, and how everyone can help each other in the future.

Family needs

Throughout the person's disorder it is important to remember the needs of other family members. Here are some practical ways family members can meet each other's needs:

- Set aside time to spend with other family members.

- Organize family outings or events where everyone can take part, for example having a meal together at a restaurant or a picnic in the park.

- Encourage family members to see the positive qualities in the family member who is unwell, not just their mental disorder. They are a person, not the disorder!

- If children are involved, ensure they keep in touch with their friends and continue to do things that other children their age are doing, for example bicycle riding or going to the movies.

- Try to do some of the enjoyable things that the family may have done before the person became unwell, such as going out for a meal, going for walks, going shopping, or going to a concert or sporting event.

Stigma and discrimination

Stigma is a broad term that describes unhelpful and stereotypical thoughts, attitudes and feelings about people based on their traits. This can include gender, skin color, sexual orientation, religion and a mental disorder. Stigma has been used to label certain groups of people as less worthy of respect than others.

There is stigma associated with having a mental disorder. This stigma can result in a person with schizophrenia being discriminated against. This means being treated differently, excluded, given fewer opportunities and denied full and equal social standing as another person.

For people with schizophrenia the stigma and discrimination associated with schizophrenia can be just as debilitating as the disorder itself. They may find that some members of the public are less likely to be supportive or empathize with them, and they may be awkward or uncomfortable around them. The media, public attitudes and unhelpful stereotypes can reinforce stigma. It is also reinforced with the use of discriminatory terms (name-calling), such as "psycho," "schizo," "nut" and "crazy."

There are two forms of stigma—public stigma and self-stigma:

- Public stigma is the reaction that the public have to people with mental disorder.

- Self-stigma is the unhelpful view that people who live with mental disorder have of themselves because of their disorder. This happens when a person fears discrimination because of having a mental disorder. It may make a person hide their disorder from others. Some unhelpful emotions that people may feel towards themselves include shame, embarrassment, alienation and fear.

Common myths, stereotypes and stigma of schizophrenia

As described in Chapter 2, some common misperceptions that contribute to the stigma of schizophrenia and mental disorder include:

- That people with schizophrenia are usually dangerous.

- That they can use willpower to stop their disorder.

- That they are unfit to work.

- That they have a "split personality."

- That schizophrenia is untreatable.

Stigma can make a person with schizophrenia:

- Feel alienated socially. Consequentially, they may lose contact with family, friends and social groups.

- Have difficulty finding or remaining in employment, gaining a promotion or completing their studies.

- Feel discouraged when it comes to seeking help. People may not understand their symptoms and be hesitant to seek treatment, often because of the unhelpful attitudes they have experienced. This can delay any treatment and recovery.

- Experience lower self-esteem and self-worth because of the diagnosis.

Ways to challenge stigma

Many organizations, such as mental health support groups and government organizations, are working together to challenge societal myths, stereotypes, discrimination and stigma associated with mental disorders. They do this by education and persuasion programs in the media and throughout the community, and by encouraging the community to have contact with people with mental disorders. The programs try to increase public and media awareness and knowledge of schizophrenia and mental illness, and use the law to act in cases of discrimination.

Challenging stigma involves a whole-hearted approach by the person, carers, friends and family, and the person's work colleagues.

The key elements in challenging stigma are:

- **Learning about schizophrenia.** Find out the facts. Having the facts can help you challenge the misinformation that leads to stigma. For example, research shows that, on average, one in five adults (17.6%) has experienced a common mental disorder within the past 12 months and around 29 percent of adults will experience a mental disorder at some stage in their lives.

- **Changing how you talk and think about schizophrenia.** Talk and think about schizophrenia like you would any other medical illness, like cancer or diabetes.

- **Challenging and informing others.** Challenge others who believe the myths and stereotypes associated with schizophrenia. Give them the facts.

- **Using the right words.** Words such as "schizophrenic," "crazy" or "psycho" are hurtful. You can refer to them as "a person with schizophrenia," or by saying, for example, "Jane is being treated for schizophrenia."

- **Being respectful.** A person with schizophrenia is entitled to the same respect and rights as any other valuable member of society.

- **Challenging the media and other organizations** that misrepresent schizophrenia and reinforce the myths and stereotypes. For instance, make a complaint to the authorities.

- **Encouraging contact.** The more contact the community has with people with mental disorder, the less likely they are to discriminate towards these individuals.

My daughter Annabel told her teenage friends off for calling their friend Penny a "psycho" and "schizo" because she had seen a psychiatrist. Annabel gave her friends the facts that about 29 percent of adults experienced a mental disorder in their lives, and told them that it was likely that one of them could have a mental disorder in their life. I was so proud of her standing up for Penny and Penny's rights.

Most importantly, challenge yourself. Change how you think and feel about schizophrenia and other mental disorders. Thought-provoking questions you can ask yourself include:

- What do I think of homeless people?

- What do I think of the government spending tax money on mental health?

- What do I think when I hear about a person with a mental disorder who has died by suicide?

The following are helpful things you and others can do to overcome the stigma:

- Become educated about schizophrenia and mental disorders in general.

- Talk openly about schizophrenia with the person, friends and family.

- Encourage the person, friends and family to read stories and personal experiences of other people with schizophrenia and mental disorder. Many websites help people to share their stories of mental disorders, including schizophrenia.

- Encourage the person to share their personal experiences with others. This may involve sharing with family and friends or via a website or Internet blog, or at a support group.

Michael was so relieved to read about other people's stories of living with schizophrenia. He did not realize that many other people experience the same things as him.

KEY POINTS TO REMEMBER

You may experience a range of mixed emotions about your supporting role. Supporting someone close to you with schizophrenia is a difficult and demanding experience that can have an impact on your overall wellbeing. However, it can also be rewarding.

Ways to improve your overall wellbeing include:

- Getting support and learning to manage stress.

- Resting, relaxing, getting enough sleep and exercising regularly.

- Finding joy in your support role.

- Planning ahead.

Every carer uses different helpful and unhelpful coping mechanisms to deal with difficult circumstances. Helpful coping mechanisms include getting support, exercising and taking time out for your caring role.

To help you cope better as a carer:

- Understand how you feel.

- Understand the disorder and the mental health system.

- Come to terms with the person having the disorder.

- Adopt an optimistic outlook.

- Set realistic expectations.

- Look after yourself.

Carers usually find it helpful to involve family and friends in the support role, to help you as well as the relative or friend you are supporting.

For people with schizophrenia, the stigma and discrimination associated with the disorder can be just as debilitating as the condition itself. Ways to overcome this stigma are to educate, challenge and encourage contact with people with the disorder.

ACTIVITY: Problem-solving

Using the problem-solving method explained in the previous chapter, try practicing solving problems about looking after yourself. First, remind yourself of the summary of the ADAPT 5-step method of effective problem-solving (see Chapter 4).

Examples of approaches to problem-solving

To help you gain a better understanding of the ADAPT 5-step method, we will first show you an example of a more helpful approach to problem-solving, then we will show you an example of a less helpful approach. The problem being worked out is related to the topic "Looking after yourself." Please remember that while some of the stages might seem difficult at first to complete, they will become much more straightforward after a while.

More helpful approach using the ADAPT 5-step method

Situation: Julie is Gary's mom and carer. Gary has been progressing well towards recovery.

Problem: Julie is feeling lonely and isolated. She misses seeing her friends.

ATTITUDE

Adopt a positive, optimistic attitude.

Julie is confident that she can make the time to see her friends and then feel less lonely and isolated.

DEFINE

Define the problem. State the facts, identify obstacles and specify a goal.

Gary has been relying less on Julie's support and assistance. Julie has many friends whom she used to see every week and would speak to on the telephone often. Since Gary became ill she has been too busy to see anyone. She has only had a few quick telephone calls with her friends. She likes getting out of the house but only has one day a week to herself.

ALTERNATIVES

Generate a list of different alternatives for overcoming the problem and achieving a goal.

1. *Julie decides to join a sewing group that meets once a week because her friends are members.*
2. *Julie calls her friends and invites them to her place.*
3. *Julie calls one of her friends and promises to call her every few days.*
4. *Julie talks to Gary and then calls her friends and arranges to meet with them on a weekly basis.*

PREDICT

Predict the helpful and unhelpful consequences for each alternative. Choose the best one to achieve your goal that minimizes costs and maximizes benefits.

Alternatives	Helpful consequences	Unhelpful consequences
Alternative 1	Julie sees her friends regularly. Julie feels less lonely and isolated.	Julie does not particularly like sewing but she wants to see her friends regularly. Julie has to make sure she puts aside time each week to see her friends.
Alternative 2	Julie gets to see her friends.	Julie does not get the chance to get out of the house. Julie still may not see her friends very often, because this is a one-off arrangement.
Alternative 3	Julie enjoys speaking to her friend on the telephone and looks forward to speaking with her regularly.	Julie does not get the chance to get out of the house.
Alternative 4	After talking with Gary, Julie gets to see her friends on a regular basis, is able to get out of the house, and enjoy herself. Julie has something to look forward to each week to help her feel less lonely and isolated.	Julie has to make sure she puts aside time each week to see her friends.

TRY OUT

Try out the solution in "real life." See if it works, and evaluate it.

Try out: *After talking with Gary, Julie contacts her group of friends and they come up with a roster of weekly dates and venues for meeting each other. After one month they have all stuck to the roster.*

Problem solved: *Yes. Julie feels less lonely and gets the opportunity to share her experiences as a carer and have others provide her with support. This better attempt at problem-solving clearly identified the problem, and dealt with one problem only. It focused on altering the carer's behavior rather than the person's, and brainstormed enough realistic alternatives. Nevertheless, it was important to talk with Gary.*

ACTIVITY: Review and reflect

Now it's your turn to practice.

Think of a problem related to the topic "Looking after yourself." First, briefly describe the situation and the problem, refer back to the key features of the ADAPT 5-step method, then complete the blank ADAPT chart.

Situation:

_____

_____

_____

Problem:

_____

_____

_____

ATTITUDE

Adopt a positive, optimistic attitude.

DEFINE

Define the problem. State the facts, identify obstacles and specify a goal.

ALTERNATIVES

Generate a list of different alternatives for overcoming
the problem and achieving a goal.

PREDICT

Predict the helpful and unhelpful consequences for each
alternative. Choose the best one to achieve your goal
that minimizes costs and maximizes benefits.

Alternatives	Helpful consequences	Unhelpful consequences

Best alternative:

TRY OUT

Try out the solution in "real life." See if it works, and evaluate it.

Try out:

Problem solved:

Here is the same problem again, using a less helpful approach to problem-solving.

Less helpful approach using the ADAPT 5-step method

Situation: Julie is Gary's mom and carer. Gary has been progressing well towards recovery.

Problem: Julie is feeling lonely and isolated. She misses seeing her friends. She feels that if Gary took his medication regularly, he would be much better and she could get out more.

ATTITUDE

Adopt a positive, optimistic attitude.

Julie is confident that she can make the time to see her friends if she can make Gary take his medication regularly.

DEFINE

Define the problem. State the facts, identify obstacles and specify a goal.

Gary has been relying less on Julie's support and assistance. Julie has many friends she used to see every week and would speak to on the telephone often. Since Gary became sick, she has been too busy to see anyone. She has only had a few quick telephone calls with her friends. She likes getting out of the house, but only has one day a week to herself. She feels that if Gary took his medication he would be much better and then she could get out more.

ALTERNATIVES

**Generate a list of different alternatives for overcoming
the problem and achieving a goal.**

1. *Julie takes control of Gary's medication, and hands it to him at dinnertime, and makes sure he swallows it.*

2. *Julie gets angry with Gary and tells him that if he doesn't take his medication, she can't see her friends.*

3. *Julie tells Gary that if he doesn't take his medication he will have to go back to hospital.*

PREDICT

Predict the helpful and unhelpful consequences for each alternative. Choose the best one to achieve your goal that minimizes costs and maximizes benefits.

Alternatives	Helpful consequences	Unhelpful consequences
Alternative 1	Julie stands over Gary to make sure he takes his medication, so she can go out more.	Gary is reluctant to take his medication and may get angry with her.
Alternative 2	Julie makes Gary take his medication, so she can go out more.	Gary takes his medication but feels guilty that he is a burden.
Alternative 3	Julie makes Gary take his medication, so she can go out more.	Gary takes his medication but feels stressed about going back to hospital. Gary's symptoms may worsen because of the added stress.

Best alternative: *Julie chooses alternative 1.*

TRY OUT

Try out the solution in "real life." See if it works, and evaluate it.

Try out: *Julie stands over Gary to make sure he takes his medication every evening.*

Problem solved: *Not really. Gary becomes angry with Julie and stops talking to her. Julie feels that she cannot leave him alone when he is like this.*

KEY POINTS TO REMEMBER

The key features of the ADAPT 5-step method are:

- Identify a problem or goal that you can work towards, rather than focusing on making someone change their behavior.

- Avoid mixing problems: concentrate on one problem at a time.

- Be specific: ensure the problem is explained clearly.

- Brainstorm sufficient alternatives, otherwise you may end up not choosing the best option.

CHAPTER 6

Supporting the Person with Schizophrenia

Introduction

Carers, family members and friends play an essential role in contributing to the wellbeing of the person with schizophrenia. As the person progresses through different phases of the disorder, your level of involvement will change. Together with the person, you will continually need to re-evaluate their needs and how best to provide support. As far as possible, the person should be an active participant in their care and treatment.

Responsibilities in providing a supporting role include:

- Providing practical and emotional support.

- Advocating for the person.

- Monitoring the person's progress and treatment.

- Promoting the person's wellbeing.

- Helping to prevent relapse.

Throughout your time with the person, it is a good idea to think optimistically about their chances of recovery and to involve them actively in their recovery. At times this may be difficult when their behavior and relationship towards you are challenging.

Please understand that it will take time for the person to progress with the treatment plan before you notice signs of recovery. You also need to be realistic about your expectations as there are different levels of recovery and relapse remains a possibility.

If possible, maintain an open relationship with the health professional to discuss treatment and any other challenges you may be experiencing.

Please be aware that some people may not want their carer involved in any aspect of the treatment of their disorder at times, or at all, particularly when they are unwell. You can discuss with the health professional how best to deal with these situations. For example, the health professional may wait until the person is well and explain to them the value of having a carer involved.

In this chapter, you will find information on how to promote the person's wellbeing, provide them with practical and emotional support, manage stress for the person and yourself, and help the person take their medication when they are reluctant to. Information on how to recognize the signs and symptoms of relapse is also given.

Improving the person's wellbeing

Jeremy used to be able to look after himself completely. He was really independent. He played sports twice a week, and had many friends he would go to visit. He often used to cook dinner for the whole family. Now I do not know how I am supposed to help him. Do I look after him as if he is a child or encourage him to take as much responsibility as possible for himself?

Improving the wellbeing of the person with schizophrenia places them in a better position to recover and be able to deal with day-to-day life. There are several ways you can encourage them to look after their overall mental, physical and emotional wellbeing.

Health

Promote healthy living. This includes encouraging and enabling the person to adopt a good sleep pattern, undertake regular exercise and healthy activities, and eat a good diet. Healthy activities include hobbies, relaxation exercises, positive social interactions and enjoyable activities.

Routines

Encouraging a daily routine and predictable schedule will enable them to anticipate stress better and minimize the chance of any surprises. Find a balance between what they are able to do and what you expect. For example, you both could come up with a list of things the person should aim to do every day or every week.

Planning

Planning for situations can help you both manage the disorder better. You can work together to develop a plan about what to do in different situations and to identify circumstances that may contribute to the person becoming stressed or emotionally upset (stress is discussed in more detail later on). For instance, keep a list of contact telephone numbers and a list of things to do when a crisis is about to happen.

Coping strategies

There are several general and specific coping strategies the person can use. Encourage the use of helpful coping strategies (as discussed in Chapter 5), such as seeking support from family, friends, professionals or other services; exercising; eating well; pursuing hobbies; or taking time out. These are general coping strategies. Specific coping strategies can be tailored to the situation. For instance, if the person does not like crowds of people, which are difficult to avoid when using public transport, recommend that they travel at off-peak times and sit near an exit, so they can leave more easily.

Group support

One of the most important things a person with schizophrenia may wish to consider is joining a support group. Such groups provide support, education and the chance to talk about their situation. They are an excellent opportunity for the person to mix with others who share the same disorder, allowing them to be themselves. There are a variety of support groups available, including:

- Formal support groups: these are facilitated by a mental health clinician; for example, support groups held at a hospital or clinic.

- Self-help groups: informal groups where everyone helps themselves and each other; for example, community groups or an established organization's online self-help group or blog.

- Informal support groups: informal groups where everyone provides support to each other; for example, a local community group that provides support to younger or older people with schizophrenia.

It may be difficult to encourage the person you are supporting to join a group because of their hesitance to meet strangers or talk about themselves. You can promote the benefits of self-help therapy and make them feel confident and comfortable about attending. You may need to go with the person initially.

Each support group is different. Try not to feel put off from attending them because you or the person did not have a good experience, but try others instead. The benefits of attending support groups outweigh those of not attending.

Self-help

Self-help treatment involves the person initiating and maintaining treatment by themselves. It is an opportunity for them to take responsibility of an aspect of their care, which will help empower them to take care of themselves. There is a range of self-help treatments available to consider. Below is a list of those that can be initiated by the person and used to help alleviate other symptoms of schizophrenia, such as stress, anxiety or depression:

- Yoga, meditation and relaxation techniques.

- Mindfulness.

- Bibliotherapy (reading self-help books).

- Acupuncture and massage therapy.

- Support groups, online communities and blogs.

- Exercise.

Safety

It is important that throughout your involvement as a carer, you and the person remain safe from harm. Fortunately, in most instances, a person with schizophrenia is not a danger to themselves or others, no more so than the general population. However, in some exceptional circumstances, the person may be a threat to themselves or others when they experience persecutory delusions or are suicidal. In these situations, you may need to take steps to ensure that items they could use to inflict self-harm or harm are inaccessible, or to ensure that the person is not put in a situation that is a threat to you or them.

Even though aggression and self-harm are not common occurrences, it is worthwhile having a plan of what to do in an emergency (you will learn more about aggression and self-harm in Chapters 16 and 18, respectively). Consider discussing this with the health professional.

Emotional and practical support

The level of emotional and practical support you provide will vary depending on how the person is progressing in the phase of the disorder. Both of you will need to come to an understanding of what they are currently able to do for themselves, what level of support they are willing to accept, and what level of support you are able to provide. For example, in the acute phase of schizophrenia, you may be required to monitor them closely throughout the day. When they progress towards the recovery phase, you will need to re-evaluate what they are able to do and what you are able to provide. For instance, if they are progressing well with treatment and showing signs of recovery, you may encourage and support them to become more independent.

You can discuss with the health professional what level of support you need to provide now and in the future. Remember that you can only do what you feel comfortable with and what you feel able to do. There are other modes of support to help you, such as other family and friends, the health professional, various mental health services and carer support workers.

Family support

Family members and friends play a central role in the recovery of the person with schizophrenia. It is important for you to encourage family members and friends to learn about how they can help them receive the best support.

There are times when family and friends can have a more helpful or less helpful effect on the person trying to recover from psychosis. They may not realize the stress or difficulties they are placing on the person who may be vulnerable. This may happen when families and friends have not been given enough information about the disorder. This may result in family and friends attempting to cope with the situation in their own way. If it can be helped, family and friends should try to avoid:

- Being overly critical.

- Being intrusive, interfering or pushy.

- Being unrealistic in their expectations of the person.

- Doing almost everything for the person.

- Treating them as much younger than their age.

- Sacrificing their own needs for the person's on a regular basis.

Table 6.1 provides examples of how families or friends may communicate in a less helpful or more helpful way with the person with schizophrenia.

Table 6.1 Examples of less helpful and more helpful communication

Less helpful communication	More helpful communication
Scott, why are you always stuck in the house? It's embarrassing having you moping around the house when friends come over. Do you not have anything better to do?	Scott, you may feel a bit better if you got out of the house more, even just for some fresh air. Would you like to come for a walk with me?
A mother who fusses around her son, never leaving him alone, constantly asking him how he is, and openly worrying about him.	A mother who supports and encourages her son to be independent and to make his own decisions.

It is normal for many families to display unintentionally "high expressed emotion" (like criticism or doing almost everything for the person). In many countries, the majority of relatives demonstrate high expressed emotion, as do many health professionals. It is the exceptional circumstances of schizophrenia and the frustrations in families that can result in their communication being less than optimal to promote the person's recovery.

Fortunately, family and friends who unintentionally say less helpful things can learn to say more helpful things. You may have to educate the family and friends and help them sort through their emotions. The best way they can relate to the person is to treat them kindly, with dignity and respect.

If family and friends are having difficulty changing their less helpful attitude towards the person, family therapy or intervention could be considered. As described in Chapter 10, high expressed emotion in the family is significantly more likely to result in the person having a relapse. Approach the health professional for further information and assistance.

Stress management

An important tool for you and the person to learn is how to deal with stress. People with a history of schizophrenia have an increased chance of a relapse if they experience too much stress. Research has shown that chronic stress can increase the risk of developing depression, anxiety, other mental disorders and physical health problems.

Common sources of stress for the person may include:

- Life changes, such as moving house, or changing jobs or schools.

- Conflict with other people or a relationship break-up.

- Work- or school-related problems.

- Ongoing concerns about money.

- Daily tasks, such as rushing to get to places, or doing too many things at once.

- Excessive worrying or having unrealistically high expectations.

- Not feeling accepted or included in the family unit.

If possible, encourage the person you are supporting to try to learn ways to manage their stress. It will help them manage a part of their disorder themselves and deal with everyday tasks better. The first step in dealing with stress is to learn how to recognize it. Each person's response to stress is different. Symptoms of stress include mental, social and physical changes. Some common symptoms that the person can look out for include:

- Sleep problems.

- Changes in appetite.

- Headaches or muscle tension.

- Poor concentration or poor memory.

- Uncharacteristic mistakes or forgotten appointments.

- Anger.

- Violent or anti-social behavior.

- Emotional outbursts.

- Increased use of alcohol and/or drugs.

- Feeling exhausted and fatigued.

When the person has learnt to recognize the symptoms of stress, the next step is to put in place ways to deal with it. There are several ways to deal with stress.

Anticipating stress

By trying to recognize in advance when stress is more likely to happen, the person can be better prepared and develop ways to control what happens. This involves planning and problem-solving the best ways to respond to the stressor (the situation or thing that causes the stress) before it occurs, or simply avoiding the stressor, as long as this does not cause more problems. For example:

> Lin gets very agitated when she has to go to appointments in the city. There are so many people rushing around and she always gets lost trying to find the offices. To lessen this stress, she could arrange to have her appointments at a time where there are fewer people around, such as in the early morning or late afternoon. It might also help if she mapped out the best route to get to the offices and bring this map with her. Alternatively, she could try to have her appointments in different offices in a less busy area and time.

Relaxation

Through relaxation, people can calm their bodies and minds, and help prevent further stress. This involves taking time out or using relaxation techniques, such as visualization or breathing exercises.

Visualization

> Manuela has difficulty getting to sleep at night. She gets anxious thinking of the things she has to do the next day and can't stop thinking about the stressful things that happened that day. To help her relax she could try a visualization exercise.
>
> This involves first closing her eyes, then imagining she is in a restful quiet place that appeals to her, such as, in Manuela's case, a quiet lake. She should then try to picture as much as she can about where she is that appeals to her, including what she can smell, taste, feel, hear and see. For example, Manuela could imagine herself walking slowly by the lake, smelling the scent of the flowers and trees nearby, hearing the lapping of the water by the lake's shore, seeing the gray color of the lake, feeling leaves crackle underfoot, and tasting the cold fresh air in her mouth. She should try to enjoy the feeling of being deeply relaxed as she slowly explores "the lake" in her mind.
>
> Then when she is ready, she should gently open her eyes to come back to the present. People who do visualization exercises for the first time sometimes fall asleep, which is good for Manuela, but if she wanted to do the exercise and not fall asleep, she should do it sitting up.

Breathing

> Jackie gets very tense when she has to spend a lot of time with certain members of her family. She knows they do not mean to add to her stress, but she can't help getting worked up sometimes. One way to help her feel better is to take a time out and do some breathing exercises. For instance, she could take a deep breath in, holding for five seconds, then release the breath for as long as possible, then repeat this process ten times. Going for a walk to get some fresh air or getting some light exercise would also help.

Realistic thinking

By thinking about things realistically, people can overcome unhelpful thoughts about themselves, others or situations. This approach involves reviewing and challenging unhelpful thoughts so people can look at their situation fairly and rationally.

> Dominic doesn't like meeting new people. He thinks they will not like him because of his illness. To help Dominic cope, before he is about to meet new people, he should remind himself that it doesn't matter whether the people like him or not and that he doesn't need anyone's approval. He should think of all of the people he likes and who like him, to remind himself that he is a likeable person.

Reducing responsibilities and obligations

Streamlining and reducing one's workload helps a person cope when stress gets too much. In close collaboration with the person, this involves reducing the person's number of daily tasks, becoming better organized, managing time better, and prioritizing and reducing responsibilities.

> Ever since Sanjeet became ill he has difficulty meeting his work demands, doing household chores, attending appointments and trying to exercise. He gets flustered and makes mistakes and cannot sleep properly at night. One way to lessen the stress for Sanjeet is if he chooses to seek help for some of these tasks, such as getting help with the household chores or reducing some of his workload.

Other strategies to reduce stress include regular exercise, eating and sleeping well, and goal-setting. The best or most appropriate stress-relieving strategy depends on the situation and the person. The person you are supporting may have to try out a number of strategies to find what works best for them.

Impaired awareness

Impaired awareness of illness is when a person does not recognize that they have a serious disorder. It is a frequent symptom of schizophrenia, like delusions or hallucinations, and can be very frustrating for carers, friends and family of the person.

A person may have partial awareness of their disorder. For example, they may be aware that they have problems, but not that these problems are related to schizophrenia.

Having impaired awareness of one's disorder can lead to risks in the person not sticking with their treatment plan.

> Johnny does not feel unwell, so he thinks he does not have to take his medication or attend the self-help groups he usually attends.

As a carer, try to understand and accept that the person may have impaired awareness that they are unwell. That is a symptom of schizophrenia. Unfortunately, unlike other symptoms of schizophrenia, at present there is no clear proven effective treatment (for example, medication) for improving a person's awareness of their disorder. Taking antipsychotic medication and participating in therapy, such as cognitive behavioral therapy, adherence therapy or psychoeducation, may have some impact. Nevertheless, the best ways to improve the person's awareness are to encourage and support them to get as well as possible and for them to participate fully in their treatment. There are many examples of people gaining awareness after more fully recovering.

Below are some suggestions for dealing with the person's impaired awareness:

- Avoid confrontation with them about their disorder. Avoid trying to convince them that they are unwell, as this may cause frustration, anger or conflict.

- Consider using different language to communicate: they may not like to use the term "schizophrenia" or "psychosis" or make references to mental disorder. You may have to agree to call their disorder something else, such as the "problems."

- Try to seek common ground when having discussions with them about their disorder. For example, they may not admit that they have schizophrenia, but they may admit that they have a problem.

- Try to concentrate on working with them towards goals, like getting a job or gaining more control over their finances.

- Try to be supportive and empathetic with their situation: try to understand what it is like not to believe you have schizophrenia when everyone else thinks you do.

- Accept that their impaired awareness is part of having schizophrenia and that this may or may not improve.

- Seek help from support services: they may have professionals who know how to work with people who have impaired awareness.

You may like to discuss any problems you are having with the health professional. You can work together to come up with a solution.

Reluctance to take medication

Sally does not take her medication properly. She takes it sometimes, but not others. I don't know if this has a bad effect on her. I don't think she believes the medication is useful.

People in general do not like taking medications, and those with medical illness or mental disorder are more likely to have problems taking prescribed medications over the long term. It is normal for people to be ambivalent about taking medications and to experiment or test out whether they "really" need medication.

For most people with schizophrenia, medication, along with psychosocial treatment, is essential for recovery. Medication not taken as prescribed is one of the most frustrating things for carers, families and friends. It is important for the person to continue taking medication to prevent symptoms returning, even when they begin to feel well.

There are different ways in which the person may not take the medication as prescribed. The person may:

- Not get the prescription on time.

- Not want to take it.

- Take the incorrect dose.

- Take it at the incorrect time.

There are many reasons why the person may not take their medication. These include:

- Co-existing substance use, for example alcohol or drug use.

- Troublesome side effects of antipsychotic medications.

- Having to take a number of drugs several times a day.

- Simply forgetting.

- Lack of understanding about the medication.

- Impaired awareness of their disorder—when they are not aware they are ill.

- Specific delusions about taking medication; for example, believing the medications are poisonous, or hearing voices telling the person not to take them.

- Previous history of not taking medications.

- Cultural beliefs, language differences or stigma about mental disorder and/or taking medication.

- Insufficient support from carers, family and friends.

- High cost of medications.

- Poor relationships with health professionals.

- The person feels that the medication has not been effective.

- Skepticism about the long-term preventative benefits of the medication.

Problems with medication taking may occur in the acute or recovery phases of the disorder, but particularly during the recovery period when the person begins to feel better and thinks medication is no longer necessary.

Problems with medication taking may be minor, such as forgetting, or major, where medication is refused. As far as possible, and together with the person, talk openly with the health professional about major problems, as they may directly affect treatment or recovery. It may also be useful to talk with the health professional if the person's attitude to taking medication has changed, particularly if they are now reluctant to take medication.

There are ways to manage medication taking. Like other problems related to the disorder, it is better if the person is self-sufficient and looks after their own medication taking. This also depends on the phase of disorder as to whether the person is able to manage alone or if help is needed. Ask the health professional how you could help in this situation.

Ways you and the person could manage medication taking

- Learn the reasons why medication is necessary, what the medication is supposed to do and what happens if the person stops taking the medication too soon.

- Encourage the person to take as much responsibility as possible for managing their medication.

- Together with the person, keep a list of the types of medications used, dosages, length of time taken and side effects.

- Encourage the person to develop a daily routine associated with taking medications. For example, they could wake up, have breakfast, brush their teeth and then take their medication.

- Use a pill organizer container (also known as a drug divider or dosette) to organize pills into correct dosages and dates required. Some health services can also arrange for a "Webster-pack" that is pre-packed with the person's medication.

- Be aware of when prescriptions need to be renewed and re-filled.

- Discard unused, old or previously prescribed medications safely. The best way to do this is to return them to the pharmacy or chemist.

Helpful things to try to do as a carer

- Calmly remind the person that the medication helps keep them well and is crucial to recovery.

- Listen to their complaints about side effects and encourage the person to discuss them with the health professional.

- If the person simply forgets to take the medication, give a gentle reminder when it is time to take it. A daily routine and pill organizer could also be used. It is important, however, that the person does not become reliant on you reminding them or physically giving them the medications, especially in the recovery phase.

Unhelpful things to try to avoid

- Nagging or threatening the person when they don't take their medication, as this can lead to a communication breakdown and loss of trust.

- Trying to trick them into taking medication; for example, by disguising it in food. The person may notice the effects of the medication and stop trusting you.

- Altering the prescribed dosage without specific instructions from the health professional.

- Supplementing the medication with herbs, vitamins or other medications without first discussing it with the health professional.

Recovery

Schizophrenia, just like any other disorder, is treatable. Most people make a good recovery, but need maintenance treatment. The pattern of recovery varies from person to person. Some people recover quickly with very little treatment. Others benefit from support over a longer period. If the person resumes regular substance use, this will almost certainly delay the recovery phase. Regular alcohol and drug use (most commonly, cannabis) may become a problem that requires treatment in itself.

> Kelevi found that for him recovery wasn't about getting back to how he was before he was ill. It was about finding a place where he was happy and able to manage his symptoms.

Recovery from the first episode usually takes a number of months. If symptoms remain or return, the recovery process may be prolonged. Some people experience a difficult period lasting months or even years before effective management of further episodes of schizophrenia is achieved. However, most people will recover and lead satisfying and productive lives. Some have one or more residual or ongoing symptoms of schizophrenia. In these instances, the person and the carer need to be observant for signs of worsening mental state or deterioration in functioning and to contact a health professional.

> Hua gradually recovered from her acute episode of schizophrenia and eventually was able to resume her studies. She still had an ongoing delusion about messages being sent to her through the Internet on her

"smart" phone, but this did not stop her using it to contact her family and friends and access Facebook. She only stopped using her telephone when she became more unwell.

Recovery can mean different things to different people. There is a difference between what medical personnel call "clinical recovery" and what non-medical personnel call "realistic recovery." Clinical recovery can be described as when the person stops experiencing the symptoms of schizophrenia. Realistic recovery can be described as when the person feels able to manage their symptoms, accepts their situation, works towards their goals and has hope for the future.

Working together with the person towards realistic recovery will better equip them to manage their disorder, feel good about themselves and be able to deal better with relapse.

Below are some guiding principles you might wish to adopt in supporting and encouraging the person as they work towards their "realistic recovery":

- Acceptance: accepting their disorder and its symptoms.

- Identity: reclaiming their identity and not feeling "labeled" by their disorder or that it dominates their life.

- Empowerment and independence: taking control of their life and responsibility for their disorder.

- Coping and self-management: developing healthy techniques to manage and cope with their disorder.

- Meaning and sense of purpose: finding and doing what is important to them and that they enjoy, and continuing to pursue their dreams and goals.

- Confidence: rebuilding confidence in themselves and appreciating themselves.

- Social connection: maintaining relationships with friends and family, and building new relationships with other people.

- Hope: realizing there is hope for recovery and having a better quality of life.

Please remember, however, that the role of the carer is highly variable here, and is dependent to a great extent on the quality of the relationship they had with the person prior to the onset of illness. In some circumstances, the carer might not be the right person to undertake this role and should not feel it is their responsibility to do so.

Relapse

Psychotic relapse means that the person's mental condition has deteriorated to the extent that signs and symptoms associated with the acute phase of the disorder have returned. Preventing relapse is vital to the person's recovery. You and the person can achieve this by detecting early warning signs of relapse, seeking help as soon as possible and sticking to the treatment plan. Generally, the earlier the person gets help when showing early signs and symptoms of relapse, the better the outcome will be.

Sticking to a treatment plan involves taking medication as prescribed, maintaining a healthy lifestyle, engaging in stress management, getting support from friends, family and services, educating themselves and others about the disorder, and taking part in therapy where prescribed. Unfortunately, even if the person sticks to the treatment plan, relapse is still possible, but the person will be in a better position to detect signs and symptoms earlier.

There are several signs and symptoms that can suggest a relapse, which may be obvious or unclear. The following two subsections describe different groups of warning signs and symptoms.

Potential early warning signs and symptoms

There are signs and symptoms that suggest a relapse may occur, or they may simply be indicators of stress. To establish which is which, you need to determine the seriousness of the signs and symptoms, taking into account how long they have been present and how much the person is affected.

Common signs and symptoms include:

- Change in sleep pattern (too much or too little).

- Feelings of anxiety.

- Agitation.

- Depressed mood.

- Difficulty concentrating.

- Social withdrawal.

- Irritability.

Definite signs and symptoms of relapse

The following are definite signs and symptoms of relapse. Please understand that these may differ from those of past episodes of schizophrenia and from person to person. In addition, not everyone experiences all of these signs and symptoms.

Common signs and symptoms include:

- Hallucinations.

- Increasing suspiciousness.

- Disorganized thoughts.

- Irrational speech.

- Changes in behavior.

- Severe mood swings.

- Deteriorating health.

- Excessive alcohol and drug use.

Relapse "picture" and relapse "plan"

The best way to deal with early warning signs and definite signs and symptoms of relapse is to make plans with the person about what to do when they have signs and symptoms of relapse. Therefore, when they start to show stress-related signs or otherwise, you both will know what to do. It is also a good idea if (together) you both discuss the best course of action to take with the health professional.

A good way to start this process is to get the person with schizophrenia, the carer and health professional together to swap "notes" and develop an individually tailored relapse "picture" and a relapse "plan." It is common practice in some countries (for example, Australia and the United Kingdom) to devise a relapse picture using the image of a thermometer (below) to highlight the person's early warning signs and symptoms and grouping them to indicate their level of severity. After devising a relapse picture, the person, the carer and the health professional can then develop a relapse plan about what they (person and carer) can do at each level.

Example of a relapse "picture"

The collection of common and more individual early warning signs, and the order in which they take place, make up the person's relapse picture.[1] Think about how the thoughts, feelings and behavior of the person you are caring for have been affected by these early warning signs.

One way of devising the relapse picture is to use the analogy of a thermometer to highlight early warning signs of relapse. The relapse picture for the person with schizophrenia may look something like the following example.

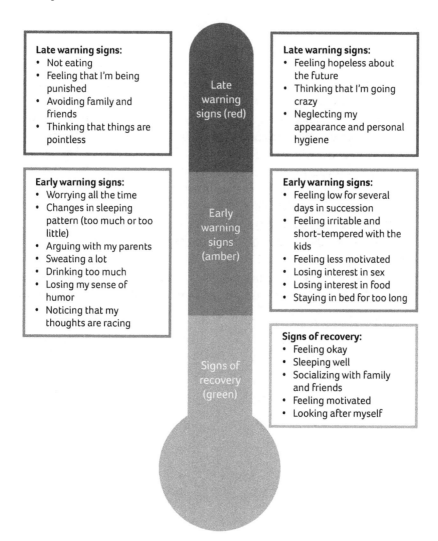

Late warning signs:
- Not eating
- Feeling that I'm being punished
- Avoiding family and friends
- Thinking that things are pointless

Early warning signs:
- Worrying all the time
- Changes in sleeping pattern (too much or too little)
- Arguing with my parents
- Sweating a lot
- Drinking too much
- Losing my sense of humor
- Noticing that my thoughts are racing

Late warning signs (red)

Early warning signs (amber)

Signs of recovery (green)

Late warning signs:
- Feeling hopeless about the future
- Thinking that I'm going crazy
- Neglecting my appearance and personal hygiene

Early warning signs:
- Feeling low for several days in succession
- Feeling irritable and short-tempered with the kids
- Feeling less motivated
- Losing interest in sex
- Losing interest in food
- Staying in bed for too long

Signs of recovery:
- Feeling okay
- Sleeping well
- Socializing with family and friends
- Feeling motivated
- Looking after myself

---

1   The relapse "picture" is adapted, with permission, from Scanlan and Manocki (2005).

Example of a relapse "plan"

Green: Support and encourage the person to use their own strategies to maintain their recovery.

Amber: Look for ways to reduce stress, increase support, practice communication skills (see Chapter 10) and encourage the person and carer to contact a health professional.

Red: Contact a health professional immediately.

Devising your own relapse "picture"

Using the same analogy of a thermometer (and together with the person with schizophrenia), write down, in order if possible, the early warning signs that make up the person's relapse picture. Remember that we all have bad days when we may feel anxious, nervous and irritable, deflated, and have difficulty sleeping. This does not mean that we are getting ill. If the person you are caring for is beginning to relapse into an acute phase of schizophrenia, you will notice clear changes in the way that they think, feel and behave over time. Do not worry if you are both struggling to identify the early warning signs, as lots of people do. A good starting point is talking to people, such as family and friends, who have been with the person when they have been unwell and well. You may find that they have noticed things that you may have forgotten.

Together with the person, the collection of common and more individual early warning signs that you have both identified, and the order in which they take place, make up the person's relapse picture. Think about how the person's thoughts, feelings and behavior have been affected by these early warning signs.

Late warning signs:

-
-
-
-

Late warning signs (red)

Late warning signs:

-
-
-
-

Early warning signs:

-
-
-
-

Early warning signs (amber)

Early warning signs:

-
-
-
-

Signs of recovery (green)

Signs of recovery:

-
-
-
-

Your relapse "plan"

Green: Support and encourage the person to use their own strategies to maintain their recovery. List the strategies to help maintain their recovery.

_____

_____

_____

_____

Amber: List the strategies to deal with early warning strategies.

_____

_____

_____

_____

Red: Contact a health professional immediately. List the additional strategies to deal with late warning signs.

_____

_____

_____

_____

KEY POINTS TO REMEMBER

- There are several ways to encourage the person to look after their mental, physical and emotional wellbeing. Your level of involvement changes as the person progresses through each phase of the disorder.

- Family and friends who have an unhelpful attitude towards the person may not realize they are causing the person extra stress. However, there are several ways for them to learn how to become supportive towards the person.

- People with schizophrenia have an increased chance of a relapse if they experience too much stress. Sticking to the person's treatment plan, detecting early warning signs and seeking help as soon as possible can also help prevent relapse. It is helpful to have a plan in place for what to do when early warning signs of a relapse occur.

- Impaired awareness is when a person is not aware they have a serious disorder. Try to accept that it is a symptom of their disorder and focus on working together towards achievable and optimistic goals.

- Reluctance to take medication is a common problem that the person and the carer experience. There are several ways to address this problem.

- Recovery from schizophrenia varies from person to person. Recovery can also mean different things to different people.

ACTIVITY: Problem-solving

This activity is an opportunity to practice solving problems related to the topic "Supporting the person with schizophrenia." First, remind yourself of the summary of the ADAPT 5-step method of effective problem-solving (see Chapter 4).

A problem has been worked out using the five steps of the ADAPT method:

Situation: Mary is Jill's mother and her main carer.

Problem: Jill does not like how she wakes up and goes to sleep at different times each day. It means Jill cannot stick to a daily routine and she gets over-tired sometimes.

ATTITUDE

Adopt a positive, optimistic attitude.

Mary believes she can help Jill to develop a better sleep routine.

DEFINE

Define the problem. State the facts, identify obstacles and specify a goal.

Jill's sleeping pattern has changed in the past month. As a result, her waking patterns have changed, she sometimes misses out on taking her medication at the right time and she is late for appointments. Jill usually doesn't like waking and sleeping at different times. She is usually independent and used to doing things her own way.

ALTERNATIVES

Generate a list of different alternatives for overcoming the problem and achieving a goal.

1. *Mary buys Jill an alarm clock to help her wake up and tell her when to go to sleep.*

2. *Mary brings Jill a cup of tea in the morning to wake her up and a glass of warm milk at night to let her know when it is time to go to bed.*

3. *After seeking Jill's suggestion, Mary buys Jill a wristwatch with an alarm, which she can set for when she wants to go to bed and wake up in the morning.*

PREDICT

Predict the helpful and unhelpful consequences for each alternative. Choose the best one to achieve your goal that minimizes costs and maximizes benefits.

Alternatives	Helpful consequences	Unhelpful consequences
Alternative 1	Jill is woken up and goes to sleep at the same time each day. Jill gets up after being woken by the alarm. Jill goes to bed when she hears the alarm.	Jill doesn't get up straight away after the alarm wakes her up. At night, Jill may not hear the alarm clock if she is not in the bedroom. Jill may ignore the alarms.
Alternative 2	Jill is woken up and goes to sleep at the same time each day.	Jill does not like to be forced to do things. Jill may ignore Mary. Jill is reliant on Mary to tell her when she has to get up and sleep.
Alternative 3	Jill is woken up and goes to sleep at the same time each day. Jill is responsible for her own waking and sleeping.	Jill may ignore the alarms. Jill may ignore Mary.

Best alternative: *Mary chooses alternative 3 because she knows Jill likes to be independent.*

TRY OUT

Try out the solution in "real life." See if it works, and evaluate it.

Try out: *After asking Jill for her suggestions, Mary buys Jill the wristwatch and Jill agrees to use it as an alarm for her to go to bed and wake up. Jill feels good about taking control of her life.*

Problem solved: *Yes. Mary and Jill are happy with how things have worked out.*

Think of a problem you are experiencing with the person you are supporting. Use this problem to practice some problem-solving. First, briefly describe the situation and the problem, then complete the blank ADAPT chart.

Situation:

_____

_____

_____

Problem:

_____

_____

_____

ATTITUDE
Adopt a positive, optimistic attitude.

↓

DEFINE
Define the problem. State the facts, identify obstacles and specify a goal.

↓

ALTERNATIVES

Generate a list of different alternatives for overcoming
the problem and achieving a goal.

PREDICT

Predict the helpful and unhelpful consequences for each
alternative. Choose the best one to achieve your goal
that minimizes costs and maximizes benefits.

Alternatives	Helpful consequences	Unhelpful consequences

Best alternative:

TRY OUT

Try out the solution in "real life." See if it works, and evaluate it.

Try out:

Problem solved:

CHAPTER 7

Young Carers

Who are young carers?

This chapter is written for children, teenagers and young adults who are supporting a parent, brother, sister, relative or friend with schizophrenia. It is also helpful if the person with schizophrenia reads this chapter, so they can understand what the young person is going through and how they can help. You do not have to be under the age of 18 to be considered a young carer.

Young carers can provide different levels of care:

- They may be the only one supporting the person (sole carer).

- They may live with the person and provide care with other people.

- They may provide care to the person, but not live with them.

Young carers provide physical and emotional support that is additional to what they would normally do for someone their age. Examples of the type of support they provide include:

- Shopping, cooking, cleaning, washing, household chores and gardening.

- Looking after brothers, sisters or relatives and their own welfare.

- Driving family members and the person to places and appointments.

- Providing translation for a family member who does not speak the language.

- Paying bills, managing banking and getting financial assistance.

- Supporting the person to take their medication and stick with their treatment plan, make appointments with health professionals and deal with emergencies.

- Encouraging and supporting the person to attend to their own personal hygiene.

- Providing emotional support—listening and providing encouragement, monitoring moods and behaviors, and being a shoulder for others to cry on.

- Keeping the person safe from harm.

These are only some of the things that young carers do.

Some young carers will provide a level of care that is inappropriate for their age. This can have an impact on their development, physical and mental health, and future prospects. Young carers of a person with schizophrenia are more at risk of their mental health and future prospects being affected because schizophrenia can be a long, drawn-out disorder.

As a young carer, you may feel that you are able to cope with the level of care you are providing, but understand that you may be at risk and, as far as possible, try to take steps to look after your own wellbeing too.

There may be specialist young carer support services that you can use. It may be difficult to speak openly about your situation and to ask for help, but it is better to do so instead of trying to cope by yourself. Being a young carer is a big responsibility, so it is important to look after your health and wellbeing first, before you attempt to support someone else.

Challenges of being a young carer

Young carers of people with schizophrenia have often been overlooked because some health professionals, mental health services and government authorities fail to recognize that children and young people are responsible for the day-to-day practical and emotional care of their parent, sibling (brother or sister), relative or friend. They forget that a person with a mental disorder may also be a parent.

Young carers face many challenges when they are supporting a person with schizophrenia. Most of these challenges are because there is less information, education and support for carers in this age group. These challenges include:

- You yourself may not realize you are a carer.

- You may not be given information about what schizophrenia is and how it affects the person you are supporting.

- You may not be given information about the person's treatment plan and about how best you can support them.

- Health professionals may not recognize that you are a carer and not include you in decision-making.

- You may have to provide mediation between your family members and friends and the person.

- You might not be informed that there are services available to support you.

- You may have difficulty finding and accessing the right support services to help you.

- You may feel guilty if you have a break or time away from the person you are supporting.

- You may not want others to know about your situation, because you are afraid of people thinking badly of you, being bullied, people treating you differently, letting the family down or being taken into care.

- You may have to accept that the person is responsible for self-managing their disorder and treatment plan, not you.

Getting support

It is extremely helpful for you to have access to a dedicated support person or group whom you can contact at any time to discuss problems or how you are feeling. This support person could be from your family (like your other parent, sister, brother, grandparent, aunt, uncle or cousin), or from a different group of people (like a friend, case manager, school counselor or guidance officer, teacher, social worker, support service representative or GP), or others you trust.

Like adult carers, as far as possible young carers should try to avoid taking sole responsibility for supporting a person, and try to obtain assistance from other family members and friends, and to access available support services.

There are a growing number of support services available that cater to young carers, and specifically young carers of a person with mental disorder. They understand what you are going through and exist to provide help, care, emotional support and information. These support services can:

- Provide confidential telephone, face-to-face or group counseling.

- Provide information about schizophrenia, including medications and treatment.

- Put you in contact with other young carers like yourself, for example a young carer support group.

- Talk to your school, university or college about the best ways to support you.

- Provide a website dedicated to young carers with an online community of young carers.

- Provide special outings and activities with other young carers where you can have fun.

- Help you access any financial assistance.

- Provide respite (a break from supporting the person); for example, by going away on a day trip or to a camp with other young carers.

Most importantly, a support service can help you find your way around the mental health service, help you understand what is happening to the person you are supporting, tell you what your rights are as a young carer and help you get access to appropriate services.

Meeting other young carers, whether face to face or via a support service's online community, can help you feel better about your situation. It is an opportunity to share your experiences with others, talk and open up about your frustrations and worries, listen to others who are in the same situation as you, learn new ways of coping and discover better ways of doing things.

Finding ways to cope

Everything that is written in Chapter 5 also applies to you as a young carer. There are several coping mechanisms to help you deal with your situation. These include:

- Getting support from services, family and friends.

- Spending time with your friends and family doing things you enjoy.

- Talking or "offloading" to others about your situation.

- Taking some time away from the person you are supporting.

- Treating yourself to something special, like going out with friends, going out for a meal or to a movie, or buying yourself a present.

- Making sure you are taking time to exercise and relax.

- Making sure you are getting enough sleep.

- Adopting a realistic and optimistic outlook about your situation and the person's disorder.

Your feelings and emotions

As a young carer, you may have a range of feelings different to adult carers. As mentioned before, talking to someone helps. Below are some examples of how you may be feeling. Remember that other young carers feel these emotions too. They are all normal reactions to situations you face.

You may be feeling stressed:

- That you have to look after the person and yourself and perhaps other people, such as younger siblings.

- That you cannot do your school work or get to school on time.

- That you are doing a lot by yourself and need help, but do not know how to get help.

It is important that you get help from other people and support services. As far as possible, avoid taking on the sole responsibility of being the support person.

You may be feeling guilty:

- That you had something to do with making the person unwell.

- That you want to get away from supporting the person.

- That it is your responsibility to make them better.

Try to understand that you did not have anything to do with the person becoming unwell, and it is not your responsibility to make them better.

You may be feeling frustrated and confused:

- That you cannot do things like other teenagers.

- That your parent, sibling, friend or relative is unwell and not like they used to be.

- That you do not have a say in what happens to the person you are supporting.

- That you do not understand what is happening to the person.

Try to understand that it is normal for you to feel frustrated about what is happening. You can still do things that you enjoy, like other children or young people your age.

You may be feeling angry and upset:

- That you are in this position.

- That the person is unwell, and things cannot be as they used to be.

Try to understand that it is normal for you to be angry and it is okay to talk about being angry to others.

You may be feeling sad and lonely:

- That you miss the way your mom, dad, sibling or relative used to be.

- That things are different between you and the person now.

- Watching what is happening to the person.

- That you have no one with whom to talk.

While it is sad what is happening to you and the person you are supporting, help is available for you and the person.

You may be feeling overwhelmed (when you feel that there are many things to do and you cannot do everything):

- That you physically cannot do everything but you want to help.

- That your feelings and emotions are making you sad and feel unhappy.

Try to understand that it is not possible to help the person all of the time. You can get help; you cannot do this role alone.

You may be feeling worried and scared:

- Watching what is happening to the person.

- That you do not know what will happen to you if the person goes into hospital or other care.

- That you will not be able to do your homework or attend school properly.

- That people or other kids will make fun of or "look down" on you and your family.

- Wondering what other people think about you and your family.

- That you might become unwell like them.

Because the person has schizophrenia it does not mean you will develop schizophrenia, too. It is scary and worrying being a young carer. If possible, talk to someone to help you deal with these feelings.

Overall, try to remember that all of the feelings and emotions you experience are normal. Do not feel ashamed. Your feelings do not mean that you love the person less. It is clear to others around you that you care deeply for the person and that you are making personal sacrifices to help them.

Juggling school or work responsibilities
At school, university or college

Young carers are likely to suffer problems at school (university, college, etc.), which the school may not realize are due to their carer's role. These problems include:

- Being late or absent regularly.
- Difficulty completing assignments on time.
- Disruptive behavior.
- Difficulty developing friendships.
- Being bullied.
- Leaving school without any formal qualifications.

If you are experiencing any of these difficulties, or if you are feeling stressed, unable to manage going to school and your support role, you and your parent or legal guardian (if possible) should speak with your school (high school/secondary school, college, university, etc.) about your situation. As mentioned above, a young carer support service may be able to help you do this, too. Generally, schools (universities, colleges, etc.) have a responsibility to look after the welfare of their students, and recognize that they are a service not just for education but for student welfare as well.

Most schools (high schools/secondary schools, colleges, universities, etc.) will have a member of staff whose job it is to support students when they are in difficulty or need help. They are often called guidance officers, chaplains, support officers or counselors. You may like to contact your school guidance officer to talk about your situation, even if you are not having any difficulties at present, but so the school is aware of your situation. It can be helpful to have someone to talk to and confide in who will listen without judging you or your family.

At work

If you are working and having difficulty juggling your support role with your work responsibilities, you could try talking with your manager or employer about your situation.

You could also access young carer support services and ask someone there to help you talk with your manager or employer. It is understandable that you may not want to discuss your personal situation with your manager or employer, but you can talk with a young carer support officer to help you figure out the best course of action.

Planning and responsibility

If possible, develop a crisis plan for what will happen if the person you are supporting goes into hospital or other care. If you are under the age of 18, you will need to plan for what will happen to you when they are away. It is essential that you discuss this with a support service's representative or a health professional, so they can guide you through this process.

As discussed throughout this book, the person with schizophrenia is ultimately responsible for self-managing their disorder and treatment. There may be times when you need to support the person more through difficult periods, which you can do with the health professional and with the help of your support person or group. As far as possible in these difficult periods, involve the person in their treatment. When the person begins to recover, encourage and support them to take increasing responsibility for self-managing their disorder and treatment plan.

KEY POINTS TO REMEMBER ─────────────────────────

- The term "young carer" includes children, teenagers and young adults. Some young carers provide a level of care that is inappropriate for their age, which may have an adverse effect on their own wellbeing. You may experience problems at school or at work.

- Helpful ways to help you cope with your situation:

  - Try to avoid taking on sole responsibility for being the support person.

  - Get support from services, family and friends.

  - Learn about the person's disorder and treatment.

  - Spend time with your friends and family doing things you enjoy.

- Take some time away from the person you are supporting.

- Continue to do the things you enjoy, like other young people your age.

- Take time to exercise and relax, and get enough sleep.

- Adopt a realistic and optimistic outlook about your situation and the person's disorder.

- As a young carer it is important that you understand that you:

  - Are not responsible for the person's disorder.

  - May sometimes feel sad, frustrated or angry about what is happening to you and the person. It is okay to talk to others about your feelings.

- If you are under the age of 18, it is a good idea to plan for what will happen to you if the person you are supporting goes into hospital or other care. The health professional and support services should be able to help you develop a plan.

ACTIVITY: Review and reflect

This activity will help you review and reflect on this chapter on young carers. Read the following scenarios for the carer and person with schizophrenia and answer the questions, taking into account what you have just read.

Mohammed looks after his dad who has schizophrenia. He regularly takes his dad to see his dad's friends, shopping and to sporting events. He also encourages him to take his medication and to eat proper meals. His mom helps him sometimes but she has poor health, so Mohammed looks after his dad mostly by himself. Mohammed did not go to school last week because his dad needed help. This happens a lot. His teachers think he does not care about school.

When the school calls to speak to his parents, his father doesn't answer the telephone because he doesn't like talking on the telephone, and if the school speaks to his mother she is too ashamed to explain that her husband is ill and Mohammed is looking after him, and that she can't care for him herself.

How would you help Mohammed? Consider what support services could do.

_____

_____

_____

Jessica is at university and shares care for her sister who has schizophrenia with her mother. She takes her sister out shopping and to the cinema frequently and takes time to sit and talk with her. Jessica just manages to do her assignments and exams on time and spend time supporting her sister, but she feels exhausted. She does not get to spend much time with her friends, and they do not know what she is going through.

How would you help Jessica? Consider what support services could do.

_____

_____

_____

CHAPTER 8

Providing Support in Different Cultures

Challenges of providing support in different cultures

Cultural and language differences can add complexity to a person's support role. Different cultures throughout the world may see and treat schizophrenia in different ways. This book has been written using attitudes in "Western" or developed countries.

Carers from all types of cultures experience the same challenges when supporting a person with schizophrenia, but carers from non-Western cultures may experience extra challenges in their role due to cultural or language differences. The main problems that these carers may experience are related to:

- Lack of information about schizophrenia that is culturally and language appropriate and difficulty accessing this information.

- Lack of support services that are culturally and language appropriate and difficulty accessing these services.

Mental health service providers are, generally speaking, aware of the cultural and language differences amongst service users. Often interpreter services are available, and information provided in different languages. However, it may be difficult to find guidelines for how to care for someone with schizophrenia that are specific to your cultural group.

Cultural differences towards schizophrenia

Different cultures may have their own set of values, attitudes and ways of coping with schizophrenia and its symptoms, which may be helpful or unhelpful in assisting you in your support role.

Helpful aspects of how different cultures think of schizophrenia include:

- Some cultures have a stronger community presence when it comes to dealing with mental disorder and stronger support networks to help carers and the person with schizophrenia. These include India, Thailand and Latin American countries, where family units are close knit and/or people typically have large families.

- Some cultures consider some symptoms of schizophrenia to be normal, and not threatening to one's health. For example, in some cultures in the Philippines, Ghana and India, and in Australian Aboriginal communities, hearing voices (auditory hallucinations) may be accepted and is not necessarily seen as a sign of mental disorder.

Unhelpful aspects of how different cultures think of schizophrenia include:

- Some cultures have an unhelpful attitude towards people with mental disorder and discriminate against them. This stigma places a burden on carers and the person and makes it difficult for them to get help and support from their family and community.

- Some cultures are fearful or ashamed of mental disorder and as a result may take steps to hide it in the family, exclude the person with schizophrenia or provide inattentive care to the person.

Please note that the above examples are not stereotypes of how other cultures view schizophrenia and mental disorder.

Together, you and the person you are supporting can speak with the health professional and/or support service representative about how to overcome any cultural differences or challenges. Some of the cultural differences you both may experience include:

- Finding it difficult to accept the "Western" reliance on medication to treat mental disorder.

- Having difficulty getting help from your family or community due to their unhelpful attitude towards schizophrenia.

- Mistrusting the services available.

- Finding it difficult discussing emotional problems with strangers.

- Having difficulty getting the information you want in your language.

- Feeling that you and the person you are supporting are isolated in the community.

- Being the only carer in the family despite other family members who could help, but the role falls to you because you are the female or the eldest.

Overall, you can try to seek help from services available, as well as family and friends, to help overcome or deal with any cultural and language barriers.

Getting help

If you have difficulty discussing personal or emotional problems with the health professional or other strangers, this is the first obstacle you may consider overcoming. This may be normal in your culture and in your family, but you can try to overcome this challenge to get the best care and treatment for the person you are supporting, and for yourself. Being able to communicate freely with the health professional and support services will help you greatly in your role.

Health professionals may not talk to carers because of perceived issues to do with confidentiality. Even though the professional is bound by confidentiality, they can still listen to the carer's concerns.

Ways you can try to overcome this obstacle:

- Remind yourself that confidentiality laws may bind the health professional you are dealing with. They cannot tell anyone about your situation or the person's situation, unless it is to another health professional dealing with the person's case, or if the person is at risk of harming themselves or others.

- Try to concentrate on the positive aspects of being able to communicate freely with the health professional, such as having a close and trusting relationship and being able to understand each other better.

- Remind yourself that you will be able to help and support the person you are supporting better if you can communicate more freely with health professionals and support service's representatives.

My husband, Santiago, has schizophrenia. I did not like talking with his mental health professional because it was my husband who was ill, so I thought my husband should have been doing the talking. I then realized that I had to get involved and talk too if I wanted to look after him properly.

If possible, try to get information about schizophrenia and its treatment in your language, and contact a carer support service and/or mental health support service that meets the needs of your cultural group. It is important that you have a contact person or organization that you can trust to help you with language or cultural barriers. You may have to try contacting a few different support services until you find one that you are comfortable with and that you believe can look after your needs.

If there is a language or cultural barrier when meeting with health professionals, consider asking for an interpreter. You may find it a great help if someone who understands your language or culture attends these meetings. Interpreters provided by the health service have to abide by confidentiality laws, just like the other health professionals.

> My son Min-jun will not go to support groups because he does not speak the language well and he does not feel comfortable sharing information with others from a different culture.

If you or the person you are supporting are having difficulty finding or accessing a support service in your language or cultural group, consider finding an appropriate service on the Internet, like an online support service, support group or "blog." This way you and the person can get some support in your language or cultural group and you do not have to reveal your personal details or meet anyone face to face.

Family support

Like other carers, it is helpful to get assistance from friends and family to share the support role. You may experience difficulty getting help if your family and the community you live in have an unhelpful attitude towards people with schizophrenia. The best way to overcome this stigma and discrimination is to educate your family and friends. One way to do this is to encourage them to read this book.

Many people know very little about the disorder. Inform your family and friends about the facts of how many people are affected by schizophrenia: approximately 1 percent of the population will experience schizophrenia. It is not a disorder only experienced by people in "Western" or developed countries. It affects people of all countries, cultures, races or religions.

> My daughter Rasheeda's illness frightened my wife. When my daughter had an episode, my wife would hide in our bedroom. She would not come out because she was too scared. So, I had to look after my daughter and look after my wife.

As a carer, challenging stigma involves a whole-hearted approach involving the person with schizophrenia, carers, friends and family, and the person's work colleagues. As described in Chapter 5, the key elements in challenging stigma are:

- Educating yourself about schizophrenia: find out the facts. Having the facts can help you challenge the misinformation that leads to stigma. For example, according to research, on average, one in five adults (17.6%) has experienced a common mental disorder in the past 12 months and around 29 percent of adults will experience a mental disorder at some stage in their lives.

- Changing how you talk and think about schizophrenia: talk and think about schizophrenia in the same way you would any other medical illness, such as lung cancer or diabetes.

- Challenging and informing others: challenge others who believe the myths and stereotypes associated with schizophrenia. Give them the facts.

- Using the right words: words such as "schizophrenic," "crazy" or "psycho" are hurtful. You can refer to the person as "a person with schizophrenia"; for example, "Ahmed is being treated for schizophrenia."

- Being respectful: people with schizophrenia are entitled to the same respect and rights as any other valuable member of society.

- Challenging media and other organizations that misrepresent and reinforce myths and stereotypes about schizophrenia: for instance, make a complaint to the authorities.

- Encouraging contact. The more contact the community has with people with mental disorder, the less likely they are to discriminate towards these individuals.

Try to explain to your family and friends that schizophrenia is treatable, most people recover, and success of treatment and recovery is dependent on their support, not just yours.

KEY POINTS TO REMEMBER

All carers of people with schizophrenia experience the same basic challenges, although the main challenges of being a carer from a different culture are:

- Lack of information about schizophrenia that is culturally and language appropriate, and difficulty accessing information.

- Lack of support services that are culturally and language appropriate, and difficulty accessing services.

Different cultures may have their own set of values, attitudes and ways of coping with schizophrenia and its symptoms, which may be helpful or unhelpful in your support role.

Mental health services and carer support services are likely to have interpreters who can help you. Try to get information about schizophrenia and its treatment in your language. You may also be able to contact a carer support service and/or mental health support service that caters to your cultural group.

It is helpful to get assistance from family and friends to share the support role.

Ways to overcome stigma and discrimination are to educate, challenge and encourage contact with people with the disorder.

ACTIVITY: Problem-solving

This activity is an opportunity to practice solving problems related to the topic "Providing support in different cultures." First, remind yourself of the summary of the ADAPT 5-step method of effective problem-solving (see Chapter 4).

A problem has been worked out using the five steps of the ADAPT method:

Situation: Adofo lives with his wife Ory and his mother, Noreen.

Problem: Noreen thinks Ory is not a good wife and believes that is why she has schizophrenia. As a result, she will not help Adofo care for Ory when he asks for help.

ATTITUDE
Adopt a positive, optimistic attitude.
Adofo believes he can get his mother to change how she feels towards Ory but understands it will take time.

DEFINE
Define the problem. State the facts, identify obstacles and specify a goal.
Noreen thinks Ory is not a good wife because she has schizophrenia. Adofo has great difficulty trying to get his mother to understand that it is not Ory's fault that she is ill. Noreen believes that Ory must have done something bad to have schizophrenia. Adofo would like his mother to learn more about schizophrenia.

ALTERNATIVES

Generate a list of different alternatives for overcoming the problem and achieving a goal.

1. *Adofo could remind Noreen of all the good things about Ory as a wife.*
2. *Adofo could give Noreen a book about schizophrenia to read.*
3. *Adofo could take Noreen to a support group for families and friends of people with schizophrenia so she could learn about schizophrenia from other people.*
4. *Adofo could take Noreen to their health professional so they could explain what the causes of schizophrenia are and assure her that Ory is not to blame for her illness.*

PREDICT

Predict the helpful and unhelpful consequences for each alternative. Choose the best one to achieve your goal that minimizes costs and maximizes benefits.

Alternatives	Helpful consequences	Unhelpful consequences
Alternative 1	Noreen remembers the good things about Ory. Noreen agrees that Ory is a good wife.	Noreen still won't know anything more about what schizophrenia is.
Alternative 2	Noreen starts to learn about schizophrenia. Noreen begins to understand that Ory is not to blame for her illness.	Noreen may not read the book.
Alternative 3	Noreen learns what other people with schizophrenia and carers experience.	Noreen doesn't like meeting new people and may be put off engaging and listening to a support group.
Alternative 4	Noreen starts to learn about schizophrenia and that Ory did not do anything wrong to develop schizophrenia.	Noreen may still not be convinced that Ory is not to blame for her illness.

Best alternative: *Adofo chooses alternatives 1, 2 and 4. He knows he needs to use many alternatives to help achieve his goal of getting his mother to learn more about schizophrenia and reinforce the message that Ory is a good wife and not to blame for her illness.*

TRY OUT

Try out the solution in "real life." See if it works, and evaluate it.

Try out: *Adofo brought Noreen to the family GP to discuss Ory and her illness. Noreen responded positively to the GP and what he said because he is someone she trusts and he comes from the same cultural background. Adofo reminded Noreen about all of the positive things about Ory, which Noreen accepted. He bought Noreen a book about schizophrenia but she has only read a few parts of it.*

Problem solved: *Mostly, yes. Noreen understands more about schizophrenia and how Ory is not to blame for developing it, but Adofo thinks everyone would benefit if she learnt more about the symptoms of schizophrenia and treatment so she could help Adofo better.*

Think of a problem you are experiencing with the person you are supporting, related to the topic "Providing support in different cultures." First, briefly describe the situation and the problem, then complete the blank ADAPT chart.

Situation:

_____

_____

_____

Problem:

_____

_____

_____

ATTITUDE

Adopt a positive, optimistic attitude.

DEFINE

Define the problem. State the facts, identify obstacles and specify a goal.

ALTERNATIVES

Generate a list of different alternatives for overcoming
the problem and achieving a goal.

PREDICT

**Predict the helpful and unhelpful consequences for each
alternative. Choose the best one to achieve your goal
that minimizes costs and maximizes benefits.**

Alternatives	Helpful consequences	Unhelpful consequences

Best alternative:

TRY OUT

Try out the solution in "real life." See if it works, and evaluate it.

Try out:

Problem solved:

CHAPTER 9

Getting the Best Out of Support Services

Getting help

To get the best out of the support services available, it is a good idea to know your rights and responsibilities and how to maintain good relationships with service providers. Ask for help when it is needed.

Many governments have produced a list of rights and responsibilities that all carers are entitled to access. The list outlines what you can and cannot do as a carer and, particularly, what you can ask and expect of support services.

You will find it extremely helpful if you are able to ask for assistance and have confidence in dealing with service providers. Remember, they have a responsibility to you too. Having a good relationship with them, especially the person's health professional, is extremely helpful to everyone. In doing this, you are all working together to achieve the same goal.

Some governments may offer financial assistance to carers of people with a mental disorder, depending on certain criteria, such as your financial position. You may find this helpful, particularly if a lot of your time is taken up with supporting the person, although please be aware that over time this payment may change or be abolished, or the eligibility requirements may change.

Please keep in mind that you play a vital role in every phase of the person's disorder. You have the right to ask questions, make complaints and get assistance. Support services are available for you, too—they are not just for the person with schizophrenia. It is helpful to check current mental health legislation, confidentiality laws, carers' rights and responsibilities, and other relevant laws and policy in your country, so you are knowledgeable on how best to access and get support from service providers.

Carers' rights and responsibilities

Many countries have a statement of rights and responsibilities for carers. In some countries, carers' rights and responsibilities are legislated. Below is a general model of carers' rights and responsibilities based on the Australian government's Mental Health Statement of Rights and Responsibilities (2012). These rights and responsibilities may vary for each country.

Carers have the right to:

- Receive respect for their human worth, dignity, privacy and confidentiality.

- Good information, education, training and encouragement to assist understanding, support and care of the person for whom they provide care.

- Receive services that help them to provide care and support.

- Give information about family relationships and any matters concerning the mental state of the person to health service providers.

- Get further opinions about diagnosis and care.

- Place limits on their availability as a support person.

- Complain to health professionals and authorities about the service, treatment or support the person is receiving and have this rectified.

- Receive help with difficulties they are experiencing because of their support-giving role.

With the consent of the person with schizophrenia, carers have the right to:

- Be consulted by health professionals about treatment options for the person and participate in treatment decisions.

- Be provided with any information that the person requests they receive.

- Request and receive information about the person's support, care and treatment.

- Contact the person while they are undergoing treatment.

- Arrange support services for the person such as respite care, counseling and community mental health services.

- Give information to those providing treatment about the general wellbeing of the person, such as their relationships with others.

Be aware that there may be times when people with schizophrenia are unable to give consent or may refuse consent because of their mental state.

Carers have a responsibility to:

- Respect the human worth and dignity of the person with schizophrenia.

- Consider the opinions of health professionals and other staff and recognize their skills in providing care and treatment.

- Cooperate, as far as possible, with reasonable programs of treatment and care aimed at returning the person to a better state of wellbeing.

Communicating with service providers

There are different types of services and support available to carers and people with schizophrenia:

- Mental health crisis services: provide support when the person requires immediate care and assessment, such as hospital inpatient units and community assessment teams.

- Community-based mental health services: community clinics and centers that have professional staff, including psychiatrists, mental health nurses, psychologists, social workers, occupational therapists and case managers, to provide assessment, diagnosis, treatment, residential care, rehabilitation and ongoing support.

- Mental health support services and carer support services: provide support for people in their recovery from mental disorder and for carers in their role. Support includes education; information; counseling; support groups; telephone helplines; Internet services, like an online support service; respite care; housing; and advocacy (support for the carer's and the person's rights).

- Financial support: financial assistance from the government for people with mental disorder and for carers (applicable in certain countries).

Accessing services

There is a range of services you and the person may like to contact and use. You can ask the health professional which services are available and look for services on the Internet or at your local community health center.

Mental health support services and schizophrenia-specific support services are available. Depending on the services available in your region or country, you can choose to access one or more services, whatever suits your needs and those of the person with schizophrenia. As a carer, try not to feel guilty about accessing these services, as they exist to support you in your support-giving role.

You may find it difficult the first time you contact a support service, as you may not know who to talk to or what information you may need to provide. It is helpful if you can explain exactly what the situation is and what type of help you are looking for. Before you contact a support service, briefly list the things you want to say; for example:

- You are a carer of a family member or friend with schizophrenia.
- Your concern or problem—keep it brief and factual.
- Information about the person's wellbeing.
- Information about your wellbeing.
- The type of assistance you need.
- When the assistance is needed.

Building relationships with service providers

It is important to build a good relationship with the person's health professional. This ensures that everyone is comfortable with each other, understands each other, is up to date with the person's progress, and that any problems are recognized and dealt with swiftly.

You can do this by asking questions, contacting the service provider when difficulties or problems arise, telling the service provider of any changes in the person's behavior or personality, and helping them when necessary.

Please understand that good relationships and communication take time and effort. Forming a positive, long-term relationship is especially important if the person's disorder is prolonged. Health professionals play an essential role in managing treatment. They are the people you are most likely to be in contact with, and are your link with other health professionals and support services.

Framework for asking questions of service providers

Feel free to ask health professionals and other service providers about the person's treatment, medication, diagnosis or anything else. As a guide, here are some questions you may wish to ask:

- What does the diagnosis mean?
- Can you explain the diagnosis in a way that I can understand?
- What types of treatment are available?
- Are the treatments helpful?
- What is my role in these treatments?
- What can I do to help?
- What can I expect in the near future and over time?
- Will they be able to continue in work or in education?
- Is it safe for them to drive?
- Will they get better?
- How often should I come and see you?
- Can you give me an out-of-hours emergency telephone number?
- Do you have any written material on this disorder? If not, who does, and is it available on the Internet?
- Is there anything that I need to change at home to make things easier or safer?
- Which mental health services should I contact for guidance and help?

As a guide, here are some questions about medications that you may wish to ask the health professional:

- Why has this particular medication been prescribed?
- How long will it take the medication to work?
- How long will they have to take the medication?
- Are there any other medications that could be used if this one does not work?
- What should I do if they experience any unpleasant side effects?
- What will happen if they stop taking the medication?
- What is my role with these medications?
- Where can I obtain written information about medications and possible side effects?

Together with the person, it is helpful if you keep a diary or record any changes in their behavior and reactions and bring this to joint meetings with the health professional. Before meetings, you also may wish to consider if there are any issues you would like to discuss, such as:

- Changes in the person's symptoms and behavior.

- Side effects of medication.

- Their general health.

- Your own health.

- If additional help is needed.

During meetings, it is a good idea to take notes and, at the end of the visit, look over your notes and tell the health professional what you both understood and what you are unsure about. This gives them a chance to correct any information or repeat something that has been missed.

Making complaints and raising concerns

There may be times when you want to raise concerns or make a complaint. Be assured that you have a right to do this. If possible, your first contact person should be a health professional.

Discuss the problem or your concerns with the health professional and ask that it be dealt with. It is best not to let too many problems build up. Try to deal with a matter as soon as it happens. It is best if you are able to help the health professionals and services handle your complaint effectively.

Consider the following steps before making your complaint:

- Clarify the complaint or concerns for yourself. Be as clear and specific as possible about the issues you want dealt with. It can be helpful to write everything down.

- Think about how best to explain your complaint or concerns. Try to focus on the issues and not the details. Ask yourself:

  - What do I want to complain or voice a concern about?

  - Why?

  - Who did it involve?

  - When and where did the issue occur?

- Keep a record of events. Your record can help health professionals identify the problem and how to address it.

- Think about what solution or outcome you want to achieve.

- Be prepared to listen to the solutions proposed and provide feedback on whether you think they will help. Ensure that the agreed solutions are included in the person's treatment plan or documented in their file.

- Always arrange a time to meet to review the agreed action, for example in one week or one month's time, so you can let the health professionals know if the solution has worked.

If the same problem arises repeatedly, or if you have alerted the health professional to a problem and nothing has happened, you could make a formal complaint. You can do this by:

- Seeking support and assistance from your local advocacy service or carer resource center (some countries have services you can access for help when making a complaint).

- Finding out who can deal with the problem. Make the complaint to that person. Ensure the person realizes you are making a complaint and that you expect a response.

- Asking about the process used to deal with the complaint: What will happen with your complaint, will you receive a written response and, if so, when?

Overall, keep in mind that it is in everyone's interest if you can work with the health professional and mental health service to deal with the concern or solve the problem. However, if you believe your complaint or concern has not been addressed properly, some countries have an ombudsman or complaints commissioner (government authority that deals with complaints) you can contact to assist with the investigation and resolution of your complaint or concern.

Confidentiality

There are two main considerations about confidentiality that affect working relationships between carers and health professionals: confidentiality laws and the trusting relationship between the person with schizophrenia and the health professional.

Confidentiality laws exist to protect the rights of people with mental disorder. Generally, health professionals have a duty of care to look after the wellbeing of the people they treat. This includes maintaining the person's privacy and ensuring all information obtained from the person is confidential. All health professionals, including administrative staff who access this information as part of the health care process, have a responsibility to maintain the confidentiality of this information.

This duty of confidentiality stops information about a person being shared with other people and organizations not involved in the health care service, unless the person's consent is given. This confidentiality does not end when the person finishes treatment or dies.

When people are accepted into a mental health service, medical records are kept about them that can be accessed by all health care workers in that particular service. Confidentiality laws control the way records can be accessed, stored and handled. In most countries, people receiving treatment are allowed to see their own medical records if they make an application in writing to the designated person in the mental health service.

In most countries, to protect the confidentiality of the person receiving treatment and comply with the relevant mental health legislation, staff are not allowed to give information to carers, other family members or friends without the person's permission. This emphasis on privacy and confidentiality for the person has led to support persons being excluded from obtaining information they need to help them in their role.

There may be exceptions to the confidentiality requirements, but it is important to check the current mental health legislation in your country. Increasingly, governments are recognizing how mental health legislation needs to acknowledge the rights of carers, specifically carers' right to information being shared with them.

Generally, if the person is under 18 years of age, they are considered a minor and information is automatically shared with their parents or legal guardians. Do not hesitate to question or challenge a health professional if you think they are not abiding by current mental health legislation. Sometimes health professionals are not up to date with changes to legislation.

Another consideration about confidentiality is that health professionals may be reluctant to talk openly with and share information with the carer about the person with schizophrenia. This is because of concerns that sharing this information with the carer might compromise the trusting relationship that has been established between the professional and the person. From these professionals' perspectives, the issue about how much information to disclose may be based primarily on clinical considerations rather than legal considerations. The important thing in this situation is for the health professional to explain this carefully and sensitively to carers.

As a carer, you may find it frustrating when you are unable to access information. Even though it is preferable that you and the person with schizophrenia attend meetings jointly with the health professional to discuss your concerns, you can still meet with the professional separately.

As a guide, health professionals may be willing to discuss with carers the following issues about the person:

- Information that is likely to be shared (for example, changes in treatment and staff).

- Circumstances when confidentiality concerns are likely to be set aside (for example, if there is a risk to the person with schizophrenia or others).

- Information that is likely to be shared in general terms, or in more detail for specific issues (for example, changes in behavior and symptoms).

As a guide, health professionals may be unwilling to discuss with carers the following issue about the person:

- Information that is not likely to be shared (for example, sexual dysfunction in the person).

Even if health professionals do not feel they can answer all your questions, this should not prevent you from giving them information you think is important.

If the person is detained under mental health legislation

In many countries, mental health legislation exists to protect the person with severe mental illness and the community. Such legislation usually provides for the assessment, detention and compulsory treatment of the person.

As a carer, your overall rights and responsibilities may be different if the person with schizophrenia is compulsorily detained. You may need to ask the mental health service, health professional or a community legal center for information and advice on your specific rights and responsibilities in relation to this form of detention.

Although legal provisions differ between and, sometimes, within countries, you may have the option to be involved in decisions about the person's assessment, detention and compulsory treatment. You also have the right to receive information about follow-up treatment (which is sometimes compulsory) when the person is about to be discharged from compulsory detention.

KEY POINTS TO REMEMBER

- To get the best out of the support services, it is helpful to know your rights and responsibilities, maintain good relationships with service providers, and ask for help.

- Many countries have produced a statement of rights and responsibilities for carers and, in some countries, carers' rights and responsibilities are legislated. Some countries' governments offer financial assistance to carers of people with a mental disorder, depending on certain criteria.

- Feel free to ask health professionals and other service providers about the person's treatment, medication, diagnosis or anything else.

- You have a right to voice your concerns or make a complaint. If possible, your first contact person should be the health professional.

- To protect the confidentiality of the person and comply with the relevant mental health legislation, staff are not allowed to give information to carers, other family members or friends without the permission of the person.

- Check the current mental health legislation, confidentiality laws, carers' rights and responsibilities and other relevant laws and policy in your country so you know how best to access and get support from service providers.

ACTIVITY: Review and reflect

This activity asks you to review and reflect on what is written in this chapter. Read the following scenario and then answer the questions.

Harold has noticed some changes in his son Blair's behavior. He has become more aggressive and withdrawn. Harold does not know if it is important, so he decides not to contact anyone about it. He does not want to bother anyone.

Do you think Harold is getting the best out of the support services? Why?

_____

_____

_____

What would you do if you were in Harold's situation?

_____

_____

_____

CHAPTER 10

Effective Communication

Importance of communication

> Mustafa does not seem to understand what I am saying when I talk to
> him. It is frustrating. I keep repeating myself, but he does not listen.
> What am I doing wrong?

Communication is the key to good relationships between the person with
schizophrenia, their carer and family. As stated earlier, schizophrenia
adversely affects the person who is unwell and may change relationships
between the person and other close friends and family. Therefore, it
is important that the family as well as the carer review how they are
communicating with each other.

Effective communication will make a difference in how everyone gets
along with each other, tackles the problems of daily living and helps the
overall recovery of the person you are supporting.

This chapter provides an overview of good communication skills, tips
on how to communicate when the person is unwell, communicating during
difficult times and the rewards of using positive language. It also discusses
the study of "expressed emotion," which highlights the importance of positive
and supportive communication from the family to promote the person's
recovery and prevent relapse.

Effective communication skills

Here are some simple and effective communication skills that you can
develop when communicating with a person with schizophrenia:

- Knowing how to communicate: check your non-verbal communication
  (tone of voice, posture, eye contact, facial expression and physical
  distance from the person).

- Listening well: by looking at the person, nodding your head or saying "uh-huh," you can show your understanding of what is being said. You can also ask clarifying questions to check what you have heard is correct.

- Checking your facial emotions: be aware that people with schizophrenia often have difficulty determining other people's facial emotions. Try not to use subtle displays of facial emotion, but make sure your facial expression clearly conveys your emotion. For example, when you are happy with the person, smile with your whole face; do not just smile a little with the edges of your mouth.

- Knowing when to communicate: try to avoid discussing things when you are upset or angry.

- Knowing what to communicate: discuss one problem at a time. Try not to overwhelm the person by giving too much information.

Communicating when the person is unwell

Conversation may be difficult when the person is unwell during the acute phase of the disorder and at times throughout the recovery phase, but there are straightforward ways to improve this.

In addition to the basic communication skills described above, here are some helpful tips you can use during these phases:

- Face the person and maintain appropriate eye contact.

- Adopt a relaxed, open posture to demonstrate that you are willing to listen. For example, do not cross your arms, put your hands on your hips, or use exaggerated movements.

- Try to keep your facial expressions calm, open and friendly.

- Do not stand too close to the person; give them some space.

- Always treat the person with respect.

- Be honest with the person.

- Avoid making promises you cannot keep.

When speaking with the person, especially during the acute phase, here are some helpful tips in addition to those described above:

- Speak in a calm, non-threatening manner.

- Be sensitive to an appropriate pace and style of interaction. At times, you may need to initiate interaction.

- Speak to the person using simple, short and clear sentences, and present one thought at a time.

- Repeat your message in different words if you think the person is having difficulty understanding you.

- Do not rush the person. It may take them time to understand completely what you are saying, and respond to you.

- Listen to their thoughts and feelings and acknowledge what they say, without interrupting.

- Be sensitive to what the person is telling you; try to see things from their perspective.

- Try to understand what is motivating the person even if what they are saying to you does not make sense.

- Take "time out" if you cannot get your message across and come back to it when you are willing to listen to each other.

- Avoid arguing with the person, no matter how logical you think your argument is, and how illogical you think their responses are.

- Convey a message of hope by assuring the person that help is available and things can get better.

When talking to the person, speak in the same way you normally speak to anyone else. The person you are supporting probably knows your personality well and is used to dealing with you. Unfortunately, when the person is unwell, they may sometimes say hurtful things. Try not to take these comments personally.

Communicating during a psychotic episode and other difficult periods

At times, it may be very difficult to communicate with the person. This is likely to happen during the acute phase of the disorder or sometimes in the recovery phase when setbacks or difficulties occur.

It is important to have a plan about what to do in this situation, and to include friends and family, if possible. The health professional can help you develop a plan. Keep in mind the following when developing your plan:

- Safety: ensure they are safe from harming themselves or others. Remove any dangerous objects nearby, such as knives, but do not try to wrestle dangerous objects from the person. Try to get them to a safe environment, such as home, a mental health unit or a hospital with an emergency department.

- Danger: if the person is at serious risk of hurting themselves or others, telephone emergency services, or use the mental health emergency numbers you have been given.

- If there is no immediate danger, contact the health professional. They will be able to assess what type of care or assistance is necessary and help you decide what to do next.

- If the person is experiencing delusions or hearing voices, avoid arguing or denying that it is happening. Remember that these are real to the person. Try to be patient and listen to what is being said. You can acknowledge how the person is feeling without agreeing with their false beliefs. This will show you are taking them seriously. Try using distraction by engaging the person in conversation about something pleasant that is based on reality (Chapter 14 discusses hallucinations and delusions in more detail).

- Your safety: remember that if you find yourself in serious risk of harm, try to get the person to a safe environment and away from dangerous objects. Remove yourself from the situation and call for help.

How quickly you need to act will depend on the severity of the situation. You will have to judge the best course of action to take on the day.

Helping the person through a psychotic episode is challenging and may be frightening or distressing to the person and to you. It may be helpful to you if you discuss your feelings with someone, such as the health professional.

Communicating using helpful language

Using helpful language towards the person you are supporting can help build their self-esteem and confidence and give them encouragement. Helpful communication means using encouraging words and supportive language, listening attentively, using a calm tone of voice and having a pleasing expression on your face. Below are some examples of helpful phrases you might wish to use:

- "You put a lot of effort into that and it's really paid off."

- "You did a great job. Well done!"
- "You've really improved on..."
- "I'm so impressed with..."
- "You just keep getting better and better."
- "Please can you help me with something? You're really good at it."
- "Thanks for your help. I couldn't do it without you."
- "That's fantastic!"
- "I trust that you can do it."

Helpful communication also involves trying to avoid using unhelpful language and not speaking in angry or harsh tones, being impatient or having an unhelpful expression on your face (for example, anger, scowling or frowning). Below are some examples of unhelpful phrases that you might try to avoid using, if you can help it:

- "Don't do that! You're not helping."
- "How many times have I told you to do that?"
- "Just let me do it by myself."
- "Why can't you just listen to me?"
- "You are hopeless at that!"
- "You should just try harder."
- "You could have done better."

Communication within the family (expressed emotion)

One way of helping to prevent relapse is that the family communicates with the person with schizophrenia in a supportive, respectful and caring way.

"Expressed emotion" is a measurement of the relationships, communication and interaction patterns between a person with mental disorder and their family. Studies have shown that people with schizophrenia living in families who display "high expressed emotion" (criticism, unsupportive, unrealistic expectations or emotional over-involvement) are more likely to relapse than people living in "low expressed emotion" (no criticism, quietly supportive and realistic expectations) households.

The problem for a person with schizophrenia when their family displays high expressed emotion is that the person not only has to deal with having a mental disorder, but also with their family's emotional over-protectiveness and criticism. This causes extra stress for the person.

There are two main characteristics of high expressed emotion:

- Emotional over-involvement: when a family member relates to the person with schizophrenia in an extremely overprotective way, with excessive emotional involvement and self-sacrifice. This has the effect of discouraging the person's skills and self-reliance. For example, a family member may say that the person with schizophrenia cannot help themselves and needs to be looked after completely.

- Criticism: critical comments made towards the person by a member of the family. For example, a family member may be critical of the person's "damage" to the overall family because they are ill.

As stated in Chapter 6, many families and health professionals unintentionally show high expressed emotion towards the person. This is due to the challenging nature of schizophrenia and the frustration in families that can result in their communication being less than optimal to promote the person's recovery. In addition, family members may not realize that their behavior is having an unhelpful effect on the person. It is often their over-estimation of what the person can easily control in terms of their symptoms, or overestimating what they (carers) need to do to protect the person and improve the effects of the disorder, which can lead to them self-sacrificing, being overly intrusive or treating the person in an age-inappropriate way.

The good news is that there are ways to improve the family environment through family intervention or family therapy, and the use of supportive, respectful and positive communication towards the person. For further information on how to improve your family's level of expressed emotion and family intervention or family therapy, talk to the person's health professional.

KEY POINTS TO REMEMBER

- Effective communication with the person you are supporting will make a difference in how the person, the family and you get along with each other; tackle the problems of daily living; and help the overall recovery of the person.

- There are simple and effective communication skills that you and the family can learn when communicating with the person.

- Together with the person, develop a plan with the health professional's help about what to do in a psychotic episode or other difficult period.

- By using positive language towards the person you are supporting, you can help build their self-esteem and confidence and give them encouragement.

- Communicating with the person in a supportive, respectful and caring way helps prevent relapse.

ACTIVITY: Problem-solving

This activity is an opportunity to practice solving problems related to the topic "Effective communication." First, remind yourself of the summary of the ADAPT 5-step method of effective problem-solving (see Chapter 4).

A problem has been worked out for you using the five steps of the ADAPT method:

Situation: Carrie is Jordan's mom and his main carer. They both live together.

Problem: For the past week, Jordan has not spoken to Carrie.

<table>
<tr><td style="text-align:center">ATTITUDE
Adopt a positive, optimistic attitude.</td></tr>
</table>

<table>
<tr><td>DEFINE
Define the problem. State the facts, identify obstacles and specify a goal.
Jordan used to speak to Carrie every day about all sorts of things. For the past month, he has spoken less and less to her. The past week he hasn't said a word to her. Carrie doesn't want to have an argument with Jordan about the problem. Carrie's goal is to attempt to re-open communication and have a short conversation with Jordan within one week.</td></tr>
</table>

ALTERNATIVES

Generate a list of different alternatives for overcoming the problem and achieving a goal.

1. *Carrie could try to initiate conversations with Jordan about topics he likes.*

2. *Carrie could speak to him regularly and include him in conversations, even if he doesn't respond, just to let him know she is there. For example, saying "hello," asking him if he wants a drink, telling him what she will do today, remarking about what is in the newspaper, and just giving him a smile.*

3. *Carrie could do nothing and allow him to be silent in the hope that he will speak to her again when he feels ready to.*

PREDICT

Predict the helpful and unhelpful consequences for each alternative. Choose the best one to achieve your goal that minimizes costs and maximizes benefits.

Alternatives	Helpful consequences	Unhelpful consequences
Alternative 1	Carrie demonstrates she wants to talk to Jordan. Jordan might speak to Carrie again.	Jordan still does not speak to Carrie. She does not know much about what he is interested in.
Alternative 2	Carrie demonstrates she wants to talk to Jordan and wishes to include him in her conversations. Jordan speaks to Carrie again.	Jordan still does not speak to Carrie.
Alternative 3	Jordan may initiate conversation by himself and speak regularly to Carrie.	Jordan still does not speak to Carrie. Jordan may feel ignored, which may only make matters worse.

Best alternative: *Carrie chooses alternative 2 because it is an informal way of engaging Jordan in conversation and it is not confrontational. She thinks it's the best way to show Jordan that she wants to talk to him.*

TRY OUT

Try out the solution in "real life." See if it works, and evaluate it.

Try out: *Carrie tried alternative 2 for one week. Jordan sometimes showed interest when she spoke to him but he didn't respond, nor did he initiate conversation with her.*

Problem solved: *No, Jordan still does not speak to Carrie.*

Think of a problem you are experiencing with the person you are supporting, related to the topic "Effective communication." First, briefly describe the situation and the problem, then complete the blank ADAPT chart.

Situation:

_____

_____

_____

Problem:

_____

_____

_____

ATTITUDE

Adopt a positive, optimistic attitude.

⬇

DEFINE

Define the problem. State the facts, identify obstacles and specify a goal.

⬇

ALTERNATIVES

Generate a list of different alternatives for overcoming
the problem and achieving a goal.

PREDICT

Predict the helpful and unhelpful consequences for each
alternative. Choose the best one to achieve your goal
that minimizes costs and maximizes benefits.

Alternatives	Helpful consequences	Unhelpful consequences

Best alternative:

TRY OUT

Try out the solution in "real life." See if it works, and evaluate it.

Try out:

Problem solved:

CHAPTER 11

Dealing with Depression

Depression is a disorder

This chapter on depression is intended for you as well as the person you are supporting. It is common for carers to experience depression as well as people with schizophrenia. The chapter aims to educate you about the symptoms of depression, the range of treatments available, and from where you can seek help.

Depression is a common mental disorder. Globally, more than 350 million people of all ages live with depression, with more women being affected than men. A person can experience depression once or multiple times throughout their lifetime. It is important to understand that depression is a treatable disorder that people can successfully manage or overcome. It is not something to be ashamed of or feel guilty about. It is not an indication of a person's character flaw, sign of weakness, or lack of discipline or personal strength. Most importantly, it is not a mood that a person can "snap out of."

It would be helpful if friends, family and the person you are supporting learn about depression. They may like to review this chapter also.

People with schizophrenia who have symptoms of depression are at a higher risk of suicide. Refer to Chapter 18 for further information on suicide.

> Emily just wants to stay in bed all day. I try to get her up, I open the curtains and promise to take her shopping and buy her some shoes, but she is not interested. Her brothers try to cheer her up. She seems to be okay during the week when she goes to school, but when she is at home, I can see that she is unhappy. Then, when I am alone, I feel very sad. I feel like I am unable to help Emily. I have not been sleeping well for a while and sometimes I want to stay in bed all day, too.

Types of depression

Clinical depression is different from a person occasionally experiencing a low mood or feeling "a bit depressed." In these cases, the person can overcome or "bounce back" from the period of depression without too much difficulty.

Clinical depression is when a person experiences symptoms of depression for two or more weeks, and their ability to function at home or at work is affected because of the depression. Symptoms can range from relatively minor (but still disabling) through to severe. Remember that depression is treatable and there are effective treatments available. A range of professional help is available to diagnose and treat depression, including GPs, counselors, psychologists and psychiatrists.

Symptoms of depression

Common symptoms of depression include:

- Feeling sad or "empty."

- A loss of interest and pleasure in normal activities.

- Changes in appetite—eating more or eating less.

- Significant weight loss when not dieting, or weight gain.

- Change in sleep patterns; for example, an inability to get to sleep or waking up early.

- Having trouble concentrating and remembering things that happened only a short time ago (short-term memory problems).

- Feeling overwhelmed by anxiety, guilt, anger, irritability or pessimism.

- Lowered self-esteem or self-worth.

- Feeling that life is not worth living (suicidal ideation).

- Less able to control one's emotions, for example anger, guilt, anxiety and irritability.

- Varying emotions throughout the day, for example feeling worse in the morning and better throughout the day.

- Reduced motivation—things do not seem worth doing.

- Lowered energy levels, for example feeling tired a lot.

- Isolation—wanting to be alone.

If you experience any of these symptoms for two weeks or more, seek help from your GP. If the person you are supporting experiences these symptoms, contact the health professional, especially if you think the depression has severe symptoms.

Treatment for depression

Depression can respond to different types of treatment. It is important for you and the person with schizophrenia to have a thorough medical assessment by your GP. This may result in you being referred to a health professional for further assessment and treatment. There are three categories of treatment: medical treatment, psychological treatment, and alternative and lifestyle treatment.

Medical treatment
Antidepressants
These are the most commonly prescribed medication for the treatment of depression. There are several types of antidepressants, with each working differently and having different uses. Not all antidepressant medications are equally effective; therefore, it is important to find the correct antidepressant for each person.

Psychological treatment
Cognitive behavioral therapy (CBT)
CBT aims to help the person change patterns of thinking or behavior that cause problems. Changing how the person thinks and behaves changes how they feel. It is a structured approach, where the person agrees goals for treatment with a therapist and tries new ways of doing things. It helps the person to think more rationally and change unhelpful patterns of thinking, emotions and behaviors associated with depression. CBT is provided by a therapist with specialized training in the approach, and has a strong evidence base as an effective psychological therapy.

Mindfulness-based cognitive therapy
Mindfulness-based cognitive therapy is a comparatively new type of psychological treatment for depression. This approach was developed to prevent relapse for those who had previously experienced an episode of depression. Mindfulness is a type of self-awareness training adapted from mindfulness meditation. It is about being aware of what is happening in the

present on a moment-by-moment basis, while not making judgements about whether we like what we find. Mindfulness-based cognitive therapy can be undertaken in a group program format or in one-on-one therapy sessions.

More information is provided about mindfulness in Chapter 3. Information is also available at the website of the University of Oxford's Mindfulness Centre.[1]

Interpersonal therapy

Interpersonal therapy is a short-term, limited-focus treatment for depression focusing on interpersonal issues. The goal of this form of therapy is to assist the person to understand how interpersonal influences are operating in their present life situation, and result in them becoming depressed and putting them at risk of future depression. Studies have found that interpersonal therapy may be at least as effective as short-term treatment with antidepressants for people with mild-to-moderate depression.

Self-help books

Reading self-help books or other materials based on CBT (for example, on the Internet on how to overcome depression) can be helpful.

Alternative and lifestyle treatment

This can include the following:

- Exercise.
- Light therapy: for seasonal winter depression, non-seasonal depression.
- Acupuncture.
- Avoiding alcohol and drugs.
- Aromatherapy.
- Consuming a nutritious diet.
- Massage therapy.
- Meditation.
- Taking omega 3 oils.
- Relaxation therapy.
- Yoga.

---

1   www.oxfordmindfulness.org

A combination of the three treatment categories may be used to treat a person's depression. For some minor forms of depression, self-help and alternative therapies may be used only.

Looking after your health and wellbeing

Looking after yourself is important. You may want to take some time out to engage in activities that give you pleasure. This will help you feel more connected with other people and places, and feel better about yourself and your relationships.

The following is a list of everyday activities that may help you to feel better:

- Meeting regularly with friends.
- Talking openly with friends about how you feel.
- Going to a movie.
- Listening to music.
- Having a relaxing soak in the bathtub.
- Walking.
- Laughing.
- Reading magazines or newspapers.
- Playing cards and board games.
- Collecting things, such as shells or coins.

What are some other things that you may enjoy?

_____

_____

_____

Looking after your health and wellbeing goes hand-in-hand with formal treatment for depression. Refer to Chapters 5 and 6 for tips on how to look after yourself and the person.

KEY POINTS TO REMEMBER

- It is common for carers and people with schizophrenia to experience depression.

- Depression is not an indication of a person's character flaw, sign of weakness, lack of discipline or lack of personal strength. Clinical depression is when a person experiences the symptoms of depression for two weeks or more, and the person's ability to function at home or at work is affected.

- A range of professional help is available to diagnose and treat depression, including GPs, counselors, psychologists, mental health nurses and psychiatrists.

- Common symptoms of depression include:

  - Feeling sad or "empty."

  - Loss of interest and pleasure in normal activities.

  - Changes in appetite and/or significant weight loss.

  - Change in sleep patterns.

  - Short-term memory problems.

  - Feeling overwhelmed by anxiety, guilt, anger, irritability or pessimism.

  - Lowered self-esteem or self-worth.

  - Less able to control one's emotions.

  - Reduced motivation and lowered energy levels.

  - Wanting to be alone.

  - Restlessness or agitation.

- If you or the person you are supporting experiences these symptoms for two or more weeks, contact your GP or the health professional, especially if you think the depression is severe or extreme. People with schizophrenia who have symptoms of depression are at a higher risk of suicide.

ACTIVITY: Review and reflect

This activity will help you review and reflect on this chapter on depression. Read the following scenarios for the carer and person with schizophrenia and answer the questions taking into account what you have just read about depression.

> Peter cares for his daughter, Charlotte, who is being treated for schizophrenia. Over the past two weeks, he has been feeling anxious that he is not providing good enough care for Charlotte. He does not sleep well, because he is worrying about Charlotte. His family has found he is becoming angry with them over little things.

How would you help Peter?

_____

_____

_____

> Elena has been diagnosed with schizophrenia, and the medication she has been taking has made her put on a lot of weight. She used to feel good about herself and her body, but now she cannot look at herself in the mirror. In the last month, she has been feeling very low about her weight and the fact that she has been diagnosed with a mental illness. She does not seem to be interested in doing the things she used to enjoy, like going shopping or to the cinema, so she stays at home a lot.

How would you help Elena?

_____

_____

_____

CHAPTER 12

Dealing with Reduced Motivation, Social Withdrawal and Sleep Problems

Reduced motivation

> Chen just watches TV all day. He says he is bored, but when I suggest places that we could go together, he says he does not want to go anywhere. Maybe he just does not want to go with me. I do not know. What can I do?

You may find at times that the person you are supporting seems to have reduced motivation or does not feel like doing anything. For example, they may stop bathing every day, seeing friends, going to work or getting out of bed. Reduced motivation is a common problem for people with schizophrenia, and is linked to a loss of interest in doing pleasurable things. This behavior is not necessarily because of anything you or anyone else has done, so try not to take it personally. The behavior is a symptom of the disorder and is not a case of the person being lazy. This behavior may be more noticeable in one phase of the disorder than others.

Reduced motivation may become serious if it persists for a long time and if it is extreme, like if the person has reduced motivation to eat. It is important to speak with the health professional in these circumstances.

There may be ways to help the person overcome or deal with this behavior, but you may not be able to change things completely. The goal is to encourage the person to manage the disorder themselves, instead of them relying on you.

Helpful tips to deal with reduced motivation

- Try to have realistic expectations of the person. Remember, this depends on what phase of the disorder they are currently experiencing.

- Encourage them to take part in simple activities that they find pleasurable, such as reading, walking, gardening, watching television, playing video games and using the Internet.

- Encourage them to initiate an activity by themselves that they will get pleasure or joy from doing.

- Work with them to break down goals and activities into simple achievable steps, so they gain confidence in doing them.

- Encourage them to develop a daily routine, for example wake up, take a shower, eat regular meals, go for a walk or listen to music.

- Appreciate them. Praise them when they do things and offer incentives or rewards. Do not be concerned if they make mistakes.

- Try to focus on the fact that they are doing something, even if they are not doing it well.

Things to try to avoid doing

- Criticizing or calling them names, such as "lazy."

- Putting pressure on them.

- Overwhelming them by giving them too many or complicated things to do.

- Asking them to do things that they are afraid of doing.

Overall, try to be patient with the person. Be flexible and realistic about what they can or cannot do. It may take time to help them feel comfortable and confident with doing things.

What is realistic to expect of the person when they have reduced motivation, and how best to communicate, can change during the different phases of the disorder. If you are unsure about what is appropriate communication considering their phase of the disorder, contact the health professional.

Social withdrawal

> Mila stays in the house every day. Most days she stays in her room. She does not even want her friends or relatives to visit her. She used to go out always to the movies, shopping, or meeting friends for dinner. Her father thinks she is sulking because of something he said.

People with schizophrenia may see themselves as different to others and feel they are unable to fit in. As a result, they may withdraw from friends and family. Social withdrawal can be a symptom of schizophrenia and/or depression.

As a carer, it is important to remember that when a person is diagnosed with a serious mental disorder, it is likely to affect their self-confidence and their sense of identity. They may lack confidence in their ability to cope in daily social situations, such as going to a supermarket or talking on the telephone. Because of this, they may cut themselves off from friends or family.

It can be difficult to know how to respond to the person if they withdraw from you and others. They can withdraw a lot or a little. For instance, they may remain in their room for weeks, eating meals in their room and only coming out to go to the bathroom, or they may spend a lot of time in their room every day, but still go outside and talk to family. Social withdrawal may occur at different phases of the disorder. It may become a serious problem if it persists and when it is extreme.

Remember that how they behave is not necessarily because of anything you or others have said or done. Coming to terms with this will help you relate better to them. Be aware that although this behavior can be puzzling or alarming, it may be helping them cope with their disorder.

As in dealing with reduced motivation, you can help the person by gradually encouraging them to take responsibility for their disorder.

Helpful tips to deal with social withdrawal

- Understand that they may feel vulnerable or lack confidence in social settings, such as going to a cinema, café, party or even a small social gathering at someone's house.

- Have realistic expectations of what they can do and are willing to do.

- Encourage them to take part in simple and undemanding social activities to help rebuild their confidence, for example going for a walk together in a calm, quiet, less visited park.

- Encourage them to take part in an activity they enjoy.

- Ask them where they would feel most comfortable.

- Encourage them to seek a quiet and safe place to withdraw to when they want to be alone.

- Listen to what they want and respect their decision to withdraw.

- Communicate with them when they stop withdrawing, for example when they come out of their room.

- Let them know you are there, if they need you.

Things to try to avoid doing

- Being pushy. Respect their wish to withdraw.

- Trying to coax them out of their room.

- Isolating them when they want to withdraw, or have withdrawn.

- Trying to force visitors on them or inviting too many visitors to the house.

- Trying to bring them to crowded social gatherings or parties.

- Attempting to prevent them leaving early if they are unable to stay long at a social gathering.

- Being overprotective by frequently asking if they want anything, or continually checking if they are okay.

- Suggesting activities or chores for them to do when they want to withdraw.

If the person is increasingly staying alone in a room, contrary to their usual behavior, this may be a sign of relapse. In this case, and if possible, notify the health professional. If you are having difficulty understanding or coping with their social withdrawal, you can also discuss this with the health professional, or with support services.

Sleep problems

> Graham hardly sleeps at night. I can hear him in the night when he walks up and down the hallway and when he watches television. He says he can't go to sleep. He says it can take hours of tossing and turning just to get four hours of sleep. I don't think it helps that he doesn't come home until very late, or that he is on his computer until after midnight.

Sleep is something people usually take for granted. Getting enough sleep is necessary to enable anybody to function properly every day. Sufficient sleep helps a person's behavior, mood, alertness, memory, problem-solving ability and overall health, as well as reducing the risk of accidents. Getting seven to nine hours of sleep per night is optimal. In reality, not everyone gets this amount of sleep, particularly people who experience schizophrenia. People with schizophrenia may have difficulty getting to sleep, going back to sleep when they wake in the night, or find they can only sleep for a few hours in the night.

There are ways to overcome disrupted sleep. To help the person you are supporting improve their sleep pattern, you could develop a sleep management plan together with them. A sleep management plan involves a good sleep routine and improving the person's sleep-related lifestyle.

Helpful suggestions for establishing a good sleep routine and sleep-related lifestyle

- Maintain a regular routine of bed times, waking-up times, meal times and the amount of activity throughout the day.

- Eat lighter meals and eat the final meal of the day in the late afternoon or early evening, not close to bedtime.

- Take ten minutes before bed to process the day's thoughts or events, and try to let go of them. It might be helpful to talk to someone about your day, or write down your feelings.

- Spend time at the end of the day winding down and trying to be calm and relaxed. You may benefit from listening to relaxing music, meditating, taking a warm bath, drinking warm milk or using mindfulness techniques.

- Exercising during the day (even 20 minutes a day) can be extremely helpful for overall wellbeing and health, and will contribute greatly towards a good night's sleep.

- Get some fresh air and spend time outdoors every day, such as reading a book or exercising.

- Avoid caffeinated and sugary drinks in the late afternoon and evening. This includes tea, coffee, cola and energy or soft drinks. Drink decaffeinated drinks from lunch onwards.

- Limit the amount of alcohol taken, especially in the evening.

- Look at your sleeping environment and consider what can be made more comfortable, for example consider room temperature, ventilation, noise, sunlight and whether the bed is comfortable.

- Avoid sleeping in late, particularly to make up for a bad night's sleep.

- Avoid overstimulation just before going to bed, such as from watching television, working, studying, searching the Internet or doing housework.

- Try to get rid of distractions. Turn off mobile phones (cell phones), computers or televisions, and let family and friends know not to disturb you.

- Avoid taking naps during the day. If a nap is really necessary, make it a short one (15 minutes) after lunch.

- If you do not fall asleep after 20 minutes, you could try getting up and doing something relaxing for a short time before attempting to go to sleep again.

- If something is troubling you, it is helpful to write down your thoughts so you can deal with them in the morning. Then you can try to sleep again.

- Don't be too worried if you cannot sleep. Worry and anxiety will reduce your ability to sleep even more. You will most likely catch up on lost sleep the next night.

The most challenging part in helping someone improve their sleep is getting them to help themselves. Try to get the person to imagine having a full night's sleep and feeling good when waking up in the morning.

Encourage them to set a goal of sticking to the sleep management plan for one week, whereby they will be rewarded afterwards. Hopefully, if this is done properly, they will notice some improvement, which will encourage them to continue with the plan.

KEY POINTS TO REMEMBER

- Reduced motivation is common in people with schizophrenia. It becomes serious if it continues for a long period of time or is extreme.

- It may be helpful if you could encourage the person to take part in simple activities that they enjoy and develop a daily routine. You could also encourage them to initiate the activity by themselves.

- People with schizophrenia may see themselves as different to others and feel they are unable to "fit in" and, as a result, may withdraw from friends and family. Try to understand they may feel vulnerable or lack confidence in social settings. Encourage them to take part in simple and undemanding social activities they enjoy to help rebuild their confidence.

- Getting enough sleep helps a person's behavior, mood, alertness, memory, problem-solving and overall health. To help the person improve their sleep pattern, it is a good idea to develop a sleep management plan together.

- Encourage the person to set a goal of sticking to the plan for one week. Hopefully they will notice some improvement, which will encourage them to continue with the plan.

- Contact the health professional or support services if you are concerned about the person's reduced motivation, social withdrawal or sleep problems.

ACTIVITY: Problem-solving

This activity is an opportunity to practice solving problems related to the topic "Dealing with reduced motivation, social withdrawal and sleep problems." First, remind yourself of the summary of the ADAPT 5-step method of effective problem-solving (see Chapter 4).

A problem has been worked out using the five steps of the ADAPT method:

Situation: Li Li cares for her son, Will, who has schizophrenia.

Problem: Will has been showing reduced motivation in doing things he usually enjoys. He used to enjoy watching and playing tennis, but since he became unwell he has stopped watching and playing the sport entirely.

ATTITUDE

Adopt a positive, optimistic attitude.

DEFINE

Define the problem. State the facts, identify obstacles and specify a goal.

Will shows a reduction in motivation in doing any recreational or social activities that he used to enjoy. Will used to play a lot of tennis and was a junior champion in the district when he was young. Now, he finds it too hard to get out of the house, let alone go to the tennis courts and play a game with his brother. He used to watch it on television on the sports channel a lot, but now he can't be bothered. Li Li would be happy if he at least started watching tennis on television again, which she believes over time would get him interested in playing tennis with his brother again.

ALTERNATIVES

**Generate a list of different alternatives for overcoming
the problem and achieving a goal.**

1. *Li Li could serve Will's meals in front of the television and make sure tennis was on.*

2. *Li Li could remind Will how much he likes tennis and how good he is at playing it.*

3. *Li Li could offer to buy him a new tennis racket and shoes if he starts watching tennis on the television and if he shows interest in playing it again.*

4. *Li Li could encourage Will's brother to be around while tennis is on the television so they have the opportunity to watch it together like they used to.*

5. *Li Li could encourage Will's brother to play tennis and invite Will to watch and take part if he liked.*

PREDICT

Predict the helpful and unhelpful consequences for each alternative. Choose the best one to achieve your goal that minimizes costs and maximizes benefits.

Alternatives	Helpful consequences	Unhelpful consequences
Alternative 1	Will watches the tennis and enjoys himself.	Will does not watch the tennis and chooses not to eat his meals in front of the television.
Alternative 2	Will remembers how much he enjoys watching and playing tennis.	Will ignores what Li Li says.
Alternative 3	Will watches and starts playing tennis again.	Will feels he is being bribed to do something he does not want to. Will does not trust his mother's intentions.
Alternative 4	Will and his brother watch tennis together. Will enjoys himself and feels encouraged to play tennis again.	Will is suspicious of why his brother wants to spend time with him. Will chooses not to watch tennis with his brother.
Alternative 5	Will enjoys watching his brother play tennis. Will decides to play tennis with his brother.	Will does watch his brother because he doesn't feel motivated to leave the house and go to the park.

TRY OUT

Try out the solution in "real life." See if it works, and evaluate it.

Try out: *Will and his brother watch tennis on the television together. Li Li gently reminds Will how good he is at tennis and how he used to play a lot. She tells him that he could still play tennis despite being ill. Over the following week Will watches tennis on the television with his brother or mother.*

Problem solved: *Yes. Will enjoys watching tennis with his mother or brother and becomes lively and animated. He has mentioned that he would like to play tennis again one day.*

Think of a problem you are experiencing with the person you are supporting, related to the topic "Dealing with reduced motivation, social withdrawal and sleep problems." What was the person like before the disorder began? How has their behavior changed? First, briefly describe the situation and the problem, then complete the blank ADAPT table below.

Situation:

_____

_____

_____

Problem:

_____

_____

_____

ATTITUDE

Adopt a positive, optimistic attitude.

⬇

DEFINE

Define the problem. State the facts, identify obstacles and specify a goal.

⬇

ALTERNATIVES

Generate a list of different alternatives for overcoming
the problem and achieving a goal.

PREDICT

Predict the helpful and unhelpful consequences for each
alternative. Choose the best one to achieve your goal
that minimizes costs and maximizes benefits.

Alternatives	Helpful consequences	Unhelpful consequences

Best alternative:

TRY OUT

Try out the solution in "real life." See if it works, and evaluate it.

Try out:

Problem solved:

CHAPTER 13

Addressing Risky Behavior

Risky behavior

> Ricky has been behaving differently to his usual self the last two weeks. He's been going out by himself and not coming home all night. The police have brought him home twice after finding him sleeping in the city. Once he came home with scratches and bruising all over his body. I'm so worried about him. I don't know what to do.

Some people with schizophrenia have difficulty assessing the risk involved when making decisions. They may have difficulty gauging the potential long-term consequences of their decision-making. This difficulty in assessing risk and its consequences can contribute to the person with schizophrenia engaging in risky behavior.

Risky behavior is when the person acts in a potentially dangerous, unsafe way, or takes lots of chances. You may find it difficult if the person you are supporting displays risky behavior.

Examples of risky behavior include when the person:

- Becomes aggressive or fights with yourself or others.

- Has thoughts of suicide.

- Stops going to work, or attending to their studies.

- Stops taking their medication.

- Spends more money than they have.

- Increases the amount of alcohol or drugs taken.

- Does not practice safe sex.

- Goes to unsafe places at night.

- Responds or acts on delusions or hallucinations, for instance thoughts of harming themselves or others.

Aggression, alcohol and drug use, not taking medication and self-harming and suicide are serious risky behaviors. These are discussed in detail in other chapters in the book (see Chapters 6, 16, 17 and 18).

Risky and vulnerable behavior

Certain types of risky behavior can make a person with schizophrenia vulnerable to ill treatment or exploitation by other people. Some people may perceive the symptoms of schizophrenia to be strange or threatening. For instance, a person who is experiencing auditory hallucinations and responds to them in a public place at night where people are consuming alcohol may be vulnerable to harassment or abuse by others.

This is because many members of the public lack knowledge of the symptoms of schizophrenia and the resulting behaviors. They may not recognize that a person displaying such symptoms has a mental disorder.

Unrestrained behavior

Unrestrained behavior is when a person is less inhibited and takes no notice of cultural norms and accepted public behavior. Examples may include when they:

- Act on impulse or act too quickly without thinking things through.

- Speak loudly or "make a scene" in a public place, even when people are looking at them.

- Are overly friendly to people, even those they have just met.

- Become very irritated by other people and their opinions.

Try to remember that although you may find some of the person's unrestrained behavior embarrassing, it may be harmless and easily tolerated.

For example, if they were being over-friendly and extremely talkative to people they just met, it may not cause any insult, harm or discomfort to anyone or to them. However, if the behavior does cause insult, harm or discomfort, you may have to deal with risky behavior.

Dealing with risky behavior

Risky behaviors may be difficult to deal with, as it is likely that the person is not aware of the behavior or that it is out of the ordinary. It may be difficult for you to find a balance between protecting the person when they display risky behavior and helping them take control.

Helpful suggestions for dealing with risky behavior when it occurs

- Communicate with the person. Let them know when their behavior is risky. Be consistent. Ensure you make them aware of their behavior each time.

- Help them to understand the consequences of what they are doing to themselves and others. You can talk to them about other people's behavior and its consequences; for instance, "Remember Jack? If he hadn't been speeding, he wouldn't have lost his driving license. Now he's going to lose his job."

- Try to distract them. This may help focus their attentions elsewhere. For example, change the subject of conversation to a neutral topic, suggest an outing they would enjoy or suggest they postpone what they want to do for another time.

- Encourage them to seek help themselves when they believe their behavior is getting out of control or is potentially harmful to themselves or others.

It is helpful to be a good role model and practice what you preach. If they see you drinking excessively or being aggressive, your message to them has less impact and you may lose their trust and respect.

When they display serious risky behavior or do extreme things that are out of character, particularly if the risk-taking puts them or other people in danger, contact emergency services or any mental health emergency numbers you may have been given first, then alert the health professional. This behavior may include:

- Physical aggression towards another person or property.

- If someone has been injured or is in need of urgent medical help.

- If your life or property is being threatened.

- If you have witnessed a crime or serious accident.

Calling emergency services can sometimes be difficult. Here are some helpful suggestions:

- Stay calm and dial the emergency number from a safe location.

- Tell the operator whether you need the police, fire or ambulance services.

- You will then be directed to an emergency operator who will take down the details of the situation.

- Stay on the line, speak clearly and answer their questions.

- Give information on where you are, including street number, name, nearest cross street and suburb/town.

- Don't hang up until the operator has all the information they need.

- If a person is unable to speak English, they just need to say "police," "fire" or "ambulance." Once connected, they should stay on the line while a translator is organized.

Things to try to avoid doing when the person displays risky behavior

- Ignoring the behavior.

- Arguing with them.

- Helping them take more risks or act out of character. For example, avoid giving them alcohol.

- Isolating or blaming them.

Remember that their actions are not because of anything you or anyone else has done. Try to remain calm if the behavior gets out of hand. Try to understand that it is the disorder that makes them behave in this way. You can also inform others close to them of the ways to deal with risky behavior. Feel free to discuss any problems you are having with the health professional or support services.

Working with the person to prevent risky behavior

Together, you and the person could try to put precautions in place to prevent risky behavior. If possible, this should be done when they are relatively well so you can get your message across more effectively. Discuss with them which precautions they can take to prevent risky behavior. This could include:

- Encouraging them to maintain a routine, such as having a regular time for going to bed, getting up in the morning, going out or doing activities and having meals.

- Encouraging them to set boundaries of what is acceptable behavior. For example, discuss with them the risky behavior that you or they are worried about, and help them identify what is acceptable behavior to them and you.

- Making them aware that there may be consequences to their risky behavior, such as getting hurt or hurting someone else.

- Minimizing stress in their life. For example, help them to avoid stressful situations, such as being in large groups of people or with certain people they find irritable (Chapter 6 discusses stress management in greater detail).

It is important that the person is involved in the decision-making process and that they feel in control of what is happening to them.

Praising good behavior

Jess decided not to buy alcohol at the shops today. I was so impressed. Usually she will pick up a bottle of wine or two when she's buying food. She didn't have any alcohol tonight either. She did so well, but when I told her so, she was dismissive. "It's no big deal Mom," she said. But I said, "No, Jess, well done—it's the little things that count."

Remember to reward good behavior and praise any achievements. Good behavior and achievements may include the person:

- Not drinking or buying alcohol or consuming illicit drugs, or choosing low-alcohol drinks.

- Saying "no" to others who want them to do something risky.

- Deciding to opt out of an activity that could be potentially risky for them.

- Continuing to take their medication on time.

- Being responsible with money.

Praise will help them feel good about themselves. It also reinforces the message that you are there to help and support them.

KEY POINTS TO REMEMBER

- Risky behavior is when the person acts in a potentially dangerous, unsafe way, or takes lots of chances. As a carer, it is important to be aware of their behavior and how it makes them vulnerable.

- Be a good role model and practice what you preach. If they see you drinking excessively, or being aggressive, your message has less impact and you may lose their trust and respect.

- When they display serious risky behavior or do extreme things out of character, particularly if the risk-taking puts them or other people in danger, contact emergency services first, then alert the health professional.

- Together, you and the person could try to put precautions in place to prevent risky behavior. These precautions could include stress management, developing a daily routine, setting boundaries of what is acceptable behavior, and making them aware that there are consequences to their behavior.

- Reward good behavior and praise any achievements.

- Discuss any problems you are having with the health professional and the person. Together, you may be able to come up with ways to help them manage their behavior.

ACTIVITY: Problem-solving

This activity is an opportunity to practice solving problems related to the topic "Addressing risky behavior." First, remind yourself of the summary of the ADAPT 5-step method of effective problem-solving (see Chapter 4).

A problem has been worked out using the five steps of the ADAPT method:

Situation: Omar's son Amir has been diagnosed with schizophrenia.

Problem: Omar is worried Amir has been taking more risks than usual. He is not taking his medication on time and is drinking alcohol until he becomes intoxicated.

ATTITUDE

Adopt a positive, optimistic attitude.

DEFINE

Define the problem. State the facts, identify obstacles and specify a goal.

The last few weeks Amir has not been taking his medication on time every day, and has missed taking it some days. Amir has also been drinking alcohol a lot more and drinks to become drunk. Omar thinks Amir has developed a low opinion of himself, as he has had schizophrenia for nine months and he wants to feel "normal" again. Omar would like to help Amir stop taking risks and encourage him to stick with his treatment so he can work towards recovery.

ALTERNATIVES

Generate a list of different alternatives for overcoming the problem and achieving a goal.

1. *Omar could discuss with Amir the consequences of not taking his medication properly and drinking too much, and help make Amir aware of how his behavior is affecting his steps to recovery.*

2. *Omar could watch over Amir as he takes his medication to make sure he takes it on time and encourage him not to drink too much.*

3. *Omar could arrange an appointment with Amir's health professional so all three of them can discuss Amir's risky behavior.*

4. *Omar could threaten Amir, and say that if he does not take his medication properly or stop getting drunk he will stop giving him money.*

PREDICT

Predict the helpful and unhelpful consequences for each alternative. Choose the best one to achieve your goal that minimizes costs and maximizes benefits.

Alternatives	Helpful consequences	Unhelpful consequences
Alternative 1	Amir understands the importance of taking his medication properly and not getting drunk. Amir understands that this risky behavior is affecting his chances of recovery. Amir takes his medication on time and stops drinking too much.	Despite listening to Omar and understanding the consequences, Amir still drinks too much and does not take his medication properly.
Alternative 2	Amir takes his medication on time and stops drinking too much.	Amir doesn't like being watched while he is taking his medication; he feels like his father doesn't trust him. Amir still drinks too much.
Alternative 3	Omar and the health professional help Amir realize the consequences of his risky behavior. Amir understands that this risky behavior is affecting his chances of recovery. Amir takes his medication on time and stops drinking too much.	Despite listening to Omar and the health professional, Amir still drinks too much and doesn't take his medication properly.
Alternative 4	Amir takes his medication on time. Amir stops drinking too much.	Amir does not like being threatened with withdrawal of money from his father. Amir still doesn't take his medication properly and drinks too much, although he has less money to spend on alcohol.

Best alternative: *Omar chooses alternatives 1 and 3. He knows that by encouraging Amir and helping him see the consequences of his actions, and this being reinforced by his health professional, will help Amir understand the severity of the risks he is undertaking.*

TRY OUT

Try out the solution in "real life." See if it works, and evaluate it.

Try out: *Over the next three weeks Omar begins to see Amir take his medication more regularly. Amir still has been drinking alcohol, but overall has not been getting drunk as frequently as before.*

Problem solved: *Yes, to some extent. Omar thinks Amir could stop drinking altogether or stop getting drunk at all. But Amir has been talking about cutting back on his drinking with Omar, as he is aware that it affects his recovery.*

Think of a problem you are experiencing with the person you are supporting, related to the topic "Addressing risky behavior." First, briefly describe the situation and the problem, then complete the blank ADAPT table below.

Situation:

_____

_____

_____

Problem:

_____

_____

_____

ATTITUDE

Adopt a positive, optimistic attitude.

↓

DEFINE

Define the problem. State the facts, identify obstacles and specify a goal.

ALTERNATIVES

Generate a list of different alternatives for overcoming
the problem and achieving a goal.

PREDICT

Predict the helpful and unhelpful consequences for each
alternative. Choose the best one to achieve your goal
that minimizes costs and maximizes benefits.

Alternatives	Helpful consequences	Unhelpful consequences

Best alternative:

TRY OUT

Try out the solution in "real life." See if it works, and evaluate it.

Try out:

Problem solved:

CHAPTER 14

Supporting the Person Experiencing Hallucinations and Delusions

Hallucinations

> Jun is talking to someone and I know there is nobody there. His younger brother is afraid. Jun isn't making any sense. I've been trying to tell him not to listen to the voices, but it's not doing any good. I think Jun is getting scared too…

Hallucinations are false perceptions, when a person sees, hears, feels, smells or tastes something that is not actually there. Most commonly, the hallucination takes the form of hearing voices (auditory hallucinations) that no one else can hear. For example, the voices may be saying they are a bad person. Other examples of hallucinations include:

- Saying they can see snakes in the room, when no snakes are there.

- Saying they can feel spiders crawling on their skin, when there are none.

Take the person seriously when they are hallucinating, as they are experiencing something that is very real to them and it may be upsetting or frightful. Everyone's experience is unique. For some, the experience of hearing voices might be comforting or positive, but for others, it might be upsetting or distressing. The voices might encourage the person to harm themselves or abuse others. The voices might start out as friendly and positive, but become unfriendly and hostile over time.

A large number of ordinary people hear voices, especially in times of tiredness; when a person is about to fall asleep or has just woken up; or in times of extreme stress, for example when a family member dies.

There is a stigma surrounding hallucinations, as with other symptoms of mental disorder. People may feel ashamed or embarrassed about hallucinations, and may even pretend to be talking on a mobile phone (cell phone) to appear normal. It may help the person you are supporting to know that many other people who experience hallucinations do not have a mental disorder.

The *Hearing Voices* approach

As mentioned in Chapter 3, there is a treatment to help people accept and deal with hearing voices, called the *Hearing Voices* approach.

The *Hearing Voices* approach is based on providing the person with coping strategies to normalize the experience. It does not aim to eliminate the voices. The approach tries to help people understand, accept and adapt to a reality that includes hearing voices, while regaining some control or power over their lives.

The approach involves the person attending a *Hearing Voices* support group with other voice hearers to share their experiences and provide the opportunity to talk freely. People who experience or have experienced hearing voices lead the groups.

If you or the person is interested in trying the *Hearing Voices* approach, you can ask the health professional and support services if there are any *Hearing Voices* support groups close to you. You can also find information on the Internet[1] and check if there are any online support groups or blogs.

The health professional should be made aware that the person is trying the *Hearing Voices* approach, so they can include it in their treatment plan.

Supporting the person experiencing hallucinations

While hallucinations can happen in any phase of the disorder, they are more likely to occur in the acute phase and during setbacks in the recovery phase.

Supporting the person experiencing hallucinations can be difficult and challenging. Fortunately, there are ways to help the person deal with them. You can help them if you:

- Accept that the hallucinations are real for the person.

- Focus on helping them reduce the distress associated with the hallucinations rather than encouraging them to get rid of them.

Then you can concentrate on helping the person deal with the hallucinations.

---

1   www.hearing-voices.org

Here are some helpful suggestions you can use to help the person deal with hallucinations:

- Stay calm.

- Empathize with them. Acknowledge their feelings attached to the hallucination. For example, say to them, "That must be frightening for you."

- Focus their attention on a distraction activity such as reading, gardening, singing, watching television or listening to music.

- Listen to what they are saying and encourage them to speak openly about the hallucination.

- Engage them in a pleasant conversation based on reality. For example, you can talk about a trip that you are about to take together, or the good results in the soccer match.

- Encourage the person to keep a diary or record when they experience the hallucinations, to help identify and avoid the situations in which they occur.

- Encourage them to be with other positive and supportive people.

- Encourage them to meet with other people who experience hallucinations. This will help them overcome feelings of isolation and the stigma associated with having hallucinations.

Things to try to avoid doing:

- Blaming yourself or others.

- Panicking or getting angry.

- Making jokes or being sarcastic.

- Asking the person to make the hallucinations stop.

- Trying to convince them that the hallucination is not real.

As well as these tips to help deal with hallucinations, it is important that the person follows their treatment plan.

If possible, contact the health professional when the person begins to experience hallucinations. If you need help during this time or just need to talk to someone, feel free to talk to the health professional or support services.

Delusions

> Gina thinks someone is coming into her room and going through her belongings when she's not there. She tells me that something has been moved or wasn't where it was supposed to be. She locks her door every time she leaves the room and gets really upset when she opens it again. I don't know what to do. I try to tell her that it's all in her head, but that only makes it worse.

Delusions are fixed false beliefs held by a person that are not held by others in their culture or religion. The person is so convinced by the delusion that the most logical argument cannot change their mind. For example, the person may believe that someone is trying to harm them, or believe that they have special powers to do things.

Delusions vary from person to person. For instance, even though it is clearly not the case, they may believe someone else is controlling their body, they are being followed or watched, or they are a movie star. The person may even develop elaborate explanations or have detailed descriptions to support their delusions.

Like hallucinations, delusions are more likely to occur in the acute phase of the disorder and during difficulties or setbacks in the recovery phase, but they may persist over long periods. Fortunately, there are ways to help the person you are supporting to cope with delusions.

Supporting the person experiencing delusions

As in supporting the person experiencing hallucinations, it can be difficult and challenging to support the person experiencing delusions. The first thing you need to overcome when trying to help the person is to accept that, to them, the delusions are real. Focus on reducing the person's distress.

Here are some helpful suggestions you can use to help the person deal with delusions:

- Empathize with them. Acknowledge their feelings attached to the belief. For example, say to them, "That must be very scary for you."

- Be patient and do not get frustrated with the person.

- Distract them by suggesting an activity they enjoy, such as reading a book or going for a walk together, or by changing the topic of conversation to something pleasant based on reality, or to a topic that the person enjoys.

- Comfort them. Reassure them that you are there to help and that they are safe.

- Encourage them to keep a diary or record when delusions occur to help identify any triggers, such as stress or anxiety.

- Take a break from the situation if you are finding it too much to bear. Ensure the person is safe from harm first.

- Engage them in conversation about something based in reality and the "here and now."

- Encourage them to try cognitive behavioral therapy to help them deal with the distress associated with the delusions.

Things to try to avoid doing:

- Convincing them that their beliefs are untrue or do not make sense.

- Joking, making fun of or being sarcastic or cynical about their beliefs.

- Confronting or challenging them about their beliefs.

- Arguing with or upsetting them.

- Pretending to agree with them.

As well as these suggestions to help support the person with delusions, it is important that they follow their treatment plan.

Remember not to take the delusions personally. They have nothing to do with anything you or anyone else has done. However, sometimes you or other family members may be included in the delusions. For example, the person may believe you or another family member is poisoning them.

If possible, contact the health professional when the person starts to experience delusions, and when you are having difficulty coping with them. Keep in mind that you can only deal with what you are comfortable with. You are not expected to cope with everything by yourself.

KEY POINTS TO REMEMBER

- Hallucinations are false perceptions that occur when a person sees, hears, feels, smells or tastes something that is not actually there. Most commonly, hallucinations take the form of hearing voices.

- Delusions are false beliefs held by a person that are not held by others or by others in their culture or religion. Hallucinations or delusions are real for the person.

- The ways you can help the person cope with hallucinations and delusions are similar. These include:
    - Empathizing with the person.
    - Focusing their attention on a distraction activity.
    - Encouraging the person to keep a diary or record when they experience the hallucinations or delusions.
    - Avoiding becoming panicked, angry, making jokes or being sarcastic.
    - Reassuring them that you are there to help, and that they are safe.

- Remember not to take the delusions or hallucinations personally. They have nothing to do with anything you or anyone else has done.

- Contact the health professional when the person starts to experience delusions or hallucinations, or if you are having difficulty coping or just want to talk. Keep in mind that you can only deal with what you are comfortable with. You are not expected to cope with everything by yourself.

ACTIVITY: Review and reflect

Consider what you have learnt above and answer the following questions.

Aldo thinks he is going to die. He thinks someone is controlling his body, making him ill, telling his body to shut down.

What would you say to him?

_____

_____

_____

Maria says God is telling her she is a good person. She is happy to hear this.

What would you say to her?

_____

_____

_____

CHAPTER 15

Dealing with Weight Gain

Weight gain

> Gavin is extremely frustrated with the amount of weight he has put on since he became ill. He's always been fit and healthy and now he can't fit into his clothes. It's affecting him really badly. I think he's getting very depressed about it...

Weight gain is a common side effect of antipsychotic medication (particularly atypical generation antipsychotics) and other problems related to schizophrenia, and is associated with increased appetite and food intake, and decreased activity. The person you are supporting is at risk of gaining weight throughout each phase of the disorder, even if weight gain has not been a problem in the past. The person may become socially withdrawn, have reduced motivation, be under-active, become depressed, or eat more food because it provides comfort.

Weight gain is a difficult problem to overcome, especially if it happens as a side effect of the medication, which is a vital part of treatment. If this occurs, consult the health professional for ways to help you both address this problem. A different medication may be prescribed that may help the person avoid gaining any (or as much) weight.

Unfortunately, weight gain may also contribute to the person feeling depressed, affect their self-esteem and affect their willingness to take their medication. There is also the risk of health problems and diseases related to gaining weight to consider, such as heart disease, diabetes, high blood pressure and some forms of cancer.

Together with the person with schizophrenia, it is important to develop a healthy eating and exercise plan that works for the person to help prevent weight gain or address it if it occurs. It may also be helpful if, together with the person, you visit a dietician to help devise a weight control or weight reduction plan.

Healthy diet

The best way to prevent or combat weight gain is to encourage and support the person to control their dietary intake and increase their amount of exercise. It is helpful if they understand the basics of what comprises a good diet. There are many different types of diets and exercise programs available that aim to give different results. The information provided below focuses on long-term healthy eating practices, which is what the person could aim for. Short-term diets are not sustainable over the time period of their disorder.

A good diet involves eating a variety of foods from the five food groups, with more emphasis on eating:

- Vegetables, legumes and beans.

- Grain (cereal) foods, such as wholegrain and high-fiber breads, cereals, rice, pasta or noodles.

- Fruit.

- Lean meats and poultry, fish, eggs, tofu, nuts and seeds.

- Milk, yoghurt and cheese.

Encourage the person to eat more vegetables and grains. Food choices that are not part of a healthy diet due to high saturated fat content, added sugars or salt or low-fiber content include:

- Alcoholic drinks: beer, wine, mixed drinks, port, sherry or liqueurs.

- Sweet treats: cakes, biscuits, sweets (lollies), pastries, chocolate and desserts.

- Foods that are high in fat or salt, or fried: crisps or potato chips, cream, processed meats, oils, "junk" foods and some takeaway foods.

- Foods with added sugar: energy drinks, fruit drinks, honey, jams, some sauces, sugar or sweetened drinks.

As far as possible, a person wishing to avoid weight gain or lose weight should try to eat or drink foods from this group rarely, and should eat them only in small amounts.

Other things the person may wish to take into account when developing their healthy eating plan include:

- Having a regular meal plan of breakfast, lunch and dinner.

- Making healthy snack choices.

- Drinking fresh water instead of sugary drinks.

- Cutting out sugar from coffee or teas.

- Cutting down the amount of oil and salt used when cooking.

- Paying attention to what food they are buying: read food labels to understand what is in the food; avoid convenience (ready-made) foods, such as meat pies, frozen meals, cooked chicken or pizza; and avoid processed foods, such as salami, sweetened cereals, muesli bars or potato chips.

- Paying attention to the size of their food portions.

- Avoiding eating quickly and stopping eating when they feel full.

- Concentrating on eating fresh foods and cooking meals from scratch. It helps if they can find simple recipes they like that they can prepare themselves.

- Avoiding eating takeaway foods, or only eating healthy takeaway options, such as sushi or salad.

- Trying to differentiate between stomach hunger (real) and psychological hunger (imagined).

The person may like to keep a diary of foods eaten. This may help them identify where they could improve their eating habits and show them when they have been eating well.

There is a lot of information on healthy eating on the Internet and published in books that the person can access.

Exercising

There are many benefits to exercise apart from preventing weight gain, assisting weight loss and improving health. These include:

- Improved sleep.

- Providing distraction from unwelcome thoughts or feelings.

- Providing an opportunity to socialize and get social support.

- Helping boost one's mood.

- Helping with one's depression.

- Helping improve one's self-esteem.

When developing their exercise plan, the person may wish to take into account the following suggestions:

- Avoid sitting for long periods of time: for example, sitting in front of a television, "smart" phone, tablet or computer.

- Increase regular physical activity. This can be at home, at a gym or outside. It is understandable if the person has reduced motivation to go to the gym or leave the house. However, there are things they can do to overcome this problem, such as using at-home exercise equipment, doing vigorous household cleaning like vacuuming, or gardening like mowing the lawn.

- Exercise with someone else or with a group. This will provide support and encouragement to continue exercising.

- Think of simple ways to exercise more, like walking to places instead of driving, parking the car further away so they have to walk further, getting off the bus one stop earlier and walking, walking swiftly upstairs, or standing and moving around while doing things instead of sitting down.

- Join a gym, sports group or club. This may depend on the person's level of health and wellbeing. Attending a gym class or playing sports once a week is helpful.

- Focus on the positives of exercise, such as improved sleep, weight loss and improved self-esteem.

It is helpful if the person works an exercise plan into their daily routine. For example, after they wake up and have breakfast they could go for a walk. You may find it useful to exercise with the person in the early stages, to help get them into a routine.

When developing the exercise plan, keep in mind that the person will have to build up their level of fitness. For example, at first they may only feel comfortable and be able to manage going for a walk once a week, then later they can increase this and work towards a goal of a certain amount of exercise per week.

You both may have to be creative in coming up with ways for them to exercise that they are comfortable with considering their disorder. For example, if they are socially withdrawn from others and don't want to go outside to see other people, you could try encouraging them to go for a walk with you in the early evening, when it is getting dark and there are fewer people around, or drive them to a quiet secluded place so they can have a walk.

Support and encouragement

As the carer, you can help by providing important support and encouragement through their diet and exercise changes, and when they stick to their plan. Try to focus on the person's achievements, such as praising them for exercising, avoiding weight gain, success in losing weight (no matter how small), or adopting a healthier lifestyle.

It is helpful if the person is in contact with others who are trying to lose weight, to share experiences and get support and encouragement. Ways to do this include becoming a member of a weight loss clinic, joining a weight loss support group or joining an online weight loss program or forum. The online method is a useful alternative if the person has difficulties mixing with new people or attending meetings.

Encourage the person to inform the health professional when they start a diet and exercise plan, to ensure it is consistent with their treatment and to ensure they can physically and mentally cope with the plan.

KEY POINTS TO REMEMBER

- Weight gain is a common side effect of antipsychotic medication and other problems associated with schizophrenia.

- If the person's weight gain is a side effect of the antipsychotic medicine, consult with the health professional to see if there is an alternative medicine they can try.

- Weight gain may also contribute to the person feeling depressed and affect their self-esteem, their willingness to take their medication, and their overall health.

- Together with the person, it is important to put in place a healthy eating and exercise plan that works for them to help prevent weight gain or reduce weight.

- It is helpful if the person incorporates an exercise plan into their daily routine. You also may find that you have to exercise with the person in the early stages to help get them into a routine.

- Most importantly as the carer, providing continual support, praise and encouragement encourages and supports them to stick to their exercise and diet plan.

- It is helpful, if they are in contact with others who are trying to lose weight, to share experiences and get support and encouragement.

ACTIVITY: Problem-solving

This activity is an opportunity to practice solving problems related to the topic "Dealing with weight gain." First, remind yourself of the summary of the ADAPT 5-step method of effective problem-solving (see Chapter 4).

A problem has been worked out using the five steps of the ADAPT method:

Situation: Irina is Alla's mom and main carer.

Problem: Alla has begun taking antipsychotic medication and has gained 5 kilograms (11 pounds).

ATTITUDE

Adopt a positive, optimistic attitude.

Irina is confident that if Alla is given good support and encouragement she will lose weight.

DEFINE

Define the problem. State the facts, identify obstacles and specify a goal.

Alla has been on antipsychotic medication for three months and has put on weight. She does not play sports. Before she took the medication she had a healthy weight and she was able to eat whatever she liked; now she eats more than she used to. Alla is frustrated at the changes happening to her body. Irina's goal is to help Alla lose weight, which, in turn, will help her feel good about herself.

ALTERNATIVES

Generate a list of different alternatives for overcoming the problem and achieving a goal.

1. *Irina encourages Alla to join a weight loss group and attend group meetings.*
2. *Irina encourages Alla to join an online weight loss forum.*
3. *Irina encourages Alla to join a gym, and go with friends.*
4. *Irina encourages Alla to take up a group sport, such as netball.*
5. *Irina helps Alla to develop a healthy eating and exercise plan.*

PREDICT

Predict the helpful and unhelpful consequences for each alternative. Choose the best one to achieve your goal that minimizes costs and maximizes benefits.

Alternatives	Helpful consequences	Unhelpful consequences
Alternative 1	Alla gets support and encouragement from other people and makes friends. Alla loses some weight. Alla learns from the program about how to control weight gain.	Alla may feel embarrassed and uncomfortable going to the group. Alla does not lose weight.
Alternative 2	Alla gets support and encouragement from other people and makes friends. Alla loses some weight. Alla learns how to control weight gain.	Alla does not engage in the online forum. Alla does not lose weight.
Alternative 3	Alla has friends who go to the gym, so they exercise together sometimes. Alla has gone to the gym in the past. Alla loses some weight.	Alla does not go to the gym. Alla does not lose weight.
Alternative 4	Alla learns a new sport and may make new friends. Alla loses some weight.	Alla does not like playing sport with people she does not know. Alla does not lose weight.
Alternative 5	Alla understands which healthy eating and exercise habits she needs to take up in order to lose weight. Alla loses some weight.	Alla does not feel motivated enough to take up the new healthy eating and exercise habits. Alla does not lose weight.

TRY OUT

Try out the solution in "real life." See if it works, and evaluate it.

Try out: *Alla agrees to go to the gym, and goes regularly. After two months she is now eating healthy food and has lost 2 kilograms (4 pounds).*

Problem solved: *Yes. Irina is happy with Alla's progress, and Alla's been feeling much better about herself.*

Think of a problem you are experiencing with the person you are supporting, related to the topic "Dealing with weight gain." First, briefly describe the situation and the problem, then complete the blank ADAPT table below.

Situation:

_____

_____

_____

Problem:

_____

_____

_____

ATTITUDE

Adopt a positive, optimistic attitude.

DEFINE

Define the problem. State the facts, identify obstacles and specify a goal.

ALTERNATIVES

Generate a list of different alternatives for overcoming the problem and achieving a goal.

PREDICT

Predict the helpful and unhelpful consequences for each alternative. Choose the best one to achieve your goal that minimizes costs and maximizes benefits.

Alternatives	Helpful consequences	Unhelpful consequences

Best alternative:

TRY OUT

Try out the solution in "real life." See if it works, and evaluate it.

Try out:

Problem solved:

CHAPTER 16

Dealing with Anger and Aggressive Behavior

Mental disorder and aggressive behavior

I get scared of George when he gets aggressive. One time he shoved me really hard into the bookcase.

Most people with mental disorder are no more aggressive or violent than anyone else. In fact, they are more likely to be the victims of violence than they are of committing violence. Unfortunately, community perceptions and the media often incorrectly portray and consider people with mental disorder as aggressive or violent.

There is, however, a small group of people with a mental disorder who may have problems with anger, controlling impulses or particular psychotic beliefs, which may make them more likely to be aggressive if they are not receiving proper treatment.

Being angry is a normal human emotion. A person's anger only becomes a problem when it turns into aggressive behavior and you, the person or others are at risk of harm. This chapter provides information on how you and the person can take steps to prevent and manage anger and aggressive behavior.

There are two main forms of aggressive behavior:

- Verbal aggression (for example, insults, threats, shouting, swearing).

- Physical aggression (for example, shoving, hitting or kicking).

If you experience aggressive behavior, try to understand that it is not necessarily a personal attack on you. This type of behavior may occur during the acute phase of the disorder or when difficulties occur during recovery. With all cases of anger and aggressive behavior it is vital that the person is taking their medication properly and following their treatment plan.

It is really hard to report violence and you may feel guilty or worry about the adverse consequences of doing so. However, it is important that you inform the health professional of any aggressive behavior so the person's treatment plan can reflect this, and you can get assistance. If you feel that you, your family or friends are in imminent danger, contact emergency services immediately.

What the person can do to manage their anger

The person can learn to recognize the physical warning signs of when they are becoming angry. These signs may include:

- Heart beating faster.

- Breathing more quickly.

- Beginning to sweat or feel hot.

- Body becoming tense or shaking.

- Feet are tapping, pacing the room, or fists are clenched.

When they recognize these warning signs, they can try some immediate strategies to lessen their anger, such as:

- Calming techniques: breathing slowly to relax their breathing, counting to 10 before reacting, or listening to calming music.

- Physical strategies: removing themselves from the person or situation that is making them angry, going for a walk or going outside for some fresh air.

- Distraction techniques: engaging in an activity they enjoy or a simple task, for instance cleaning their room.

There are also long-term strategies that the person can try to help with their anger management, which include:

- Learning relaxation techniques: yoga, meditation, mindfulness or breathing techniques.

- Learning assertiveness skills: learning to channel anger and express it in clear and respectful ways (this can be done through self-help books or attending courses).

- Engaging in anger management therapy: group therapy, peer support, counseling or cognitive behavioral therapy.

Factors contributing to aggressive behavior

As a carer, it is helpful to be aware of the factors that may contribute to a person with schizophrenia becoming angry or aggressive. These include the person:

- Experiencing hallucinations or delusions, especially feelings of paranoia.

- Feeling confused or frustrated about something or someone.

- Using alcohol or drugs.

- Experiencing stress and tension.

- Having a previous history of aggression.

Research has found that people with schizophrenia have difficulty interpreting other people's facial expressions, understanding other people's motives and understanding the subtle differences in social interactions, for example your body position. This may lead them to misinterpret what a person is trying to say or do and cause confusion, frustration or conflict, which may lead to anger.

Examples of this misinterpretation may include when they think they are being ridiculed when something is meant as a joke, when they feel challenged, threatened or "cornered" when they are not, or when they exaggerate another person's irritability and misread it as anger.

Preventing aggressive behavior

Here are some suggestions to help prevent the person becoming aggressive:

- Watch for signs that they are about to become angry or hostile. For example, you may observe tenseness, clenched fists, arguing or swearing.

- Try to stay calm. If you become angry or hostile, the problem may get worse.

- Try to calm them by distraction, for instance by changing the topic of conversation.

- Encourage them to take "time out" or a break. If this does not work, remove yourself, other people or anything that causes them to get angry.

- When they are upset, avoid arguing with them.

- Encourage them to talk calmly about what is bothering them and how they are feeling.

- Do not tease, blame, confront or ridicule them.

- Avoid raising your voice or talking too fast.

- Try to minimize any stress they are experiencing.

- Make their home or room a relaxing environment, by reducing noise levels, dimming bright lights and ensuring the temperature is comfortable.

- Limit choices. Instead of asking "What would you like to do today?" it would be better to provide them with alternatives to choose from. For example, ask them if they would rather go to the museum or visit a friend.

- Be aware if there are any particular times of the day when they become upset or frustrated.

If the person has a history of aggressive behavior, discuss this with the health professional to work out ways to anticipate and deal with the behavior. This may include removing dangerous objects from the home. If you are worried about your safety or health, make sure you have a "safe room" in the house with a lock on the door and a telephone so you or others can call for help.

Responding to aggressive behavior

Here are things you can do when the person is aggressive:

- If you can, try to calm the person down. For example, ask the person to relax. Convey a sense of hope by saying that things will be alright and use a soothing, calm voice.

- Otherwise, tell the person clearly and calmly but in a friendly voice (without shouting) to stop what they are doing, such as "stop that now, please."

- Speak clearly and slowly, in short sentences. Reassure them that you support them. Maintain a large distance between you and the person.

- Explain that once the person has calmed down, you will listen to what they have to say or help with whatever is needed.

- Try to distract them, for example by changing the topic.

- Do not attempt to handle the person physically or restrict the person's movement, for example if they want to pace up and down the room.

- Get help from others around you, if possible. Do not try to reason with the person by yourself.

- Remove yourself and other people from nearby if the behavior is too much to bear.

- Do not hesitate to telephone the emergency services or any mental health emergency numbers you may have been given.

Never compromise your own or others' safety because of concerns about hurting the person's feelings, as later they might feel very relieved that they were prevented from hurting someone. Make sure you are safe first and then contact the emergency services.

After the incident

It is important to speak to the person after the incident when things have calmed down. Say something like:

- "I know you were very upset and angry, but you do not have the right to threaten anyone."

- "You cannot be aggressive with us, ever."

- "We will not accept that sort of behavior."

It should be emphasized that you and others will not tolerate aggressive behavior, and that the person should seek help for their behavior.

As described earlier, there are long-term anger management strategies that the person could try such as anger management therapy, relaxation techniques and assertiveness skills.

Identifying triggers

It will be extremely helpful if you and the person work together to identify the triggers that set off their aggressive behavior. These triggers could be:

- Different situations, such as public places, or places with lots of people.

- Certain people, such as an unwelcome friend or family member.

- Certain activities, such as watching the news on television.

- Certain times of day, such as in the evening when they are tired.

- Dependent on their emotional state, such as when they feel stressed, misunderstood, frustrated, threatened, hurt, confused or vulnerable.

- Not taking their medication properly.

- Using alcohol or drugs.

- Symptoms of the disorder, such as hallucinations or delusions.

Once the triggers have been identified, you may be able to discuss with them the best ways to avoid them. It is important that the person takes responsibility for their actions and that they are made aware of the consequences of their behavior when they don't avoid the triggers and/or become aggressive. These consequences could be a lack of trust between you and them, a step back in their treatment, harming someone or themselves and, at the extreme, being charged with assaulting someone or being hospitalized.

As the carer, you are not expected to cope with these sorts of situations by yourself. There are people who can help and are willing to listen if you need to talk, such as the health professional, telephone support services or specialist anti-violence organizations. These professionals are all trained in dealing with these types of situations and have strict confidentiality rules to prioritize your safety.

KEY POINTS TO REMEMBER

- A small group of people with mental disorder have problems with anger, controlling impulses, or feelings of paranoia. These problems may make them more likely to be aggressive if they are not receiving proper treatment.

- With all cases of anger and aggressive behavior it is important that the person takes their medication properly and follows their treatment plan. It is important to discuss any history of aggressive behavior with the health professional.

- When the person displays aggressive behavior, you may be able to:

  - Try to calm the person down.

  - Tell the person clearly and calmly to stop what they are doing.

  - Try to distract them, but do not attempt to physically restrain them.

  - Get help from others around you, if possible.

- Help the person identify the triggers that set off their aggressive behavior and make them aware of the consequences that will occur when they don't avoid the triggers and/or become aggressive.

- As the carer, you are not expected to cope with these sorts of situations by yourself. Feel free to contact the health professional, other health professionals, telephone support services or specialist anti-violence organizations.

ACTIVITY: Behavior diary

It may be helpful to keep a diary of when the person displays aggressive behavior, so you can record any triggers to the person's anger, and take note of any helpful or unhelpful things you or others did to help the situation.

Here is an example of a simple behavior diary:

What happened?	What have I tried before?		What will I do in the future?
	What worked?	What didn't work?	
Jim became angry when he talked about his school friends who were doing well in their careers and he wished he could be normal and get on with his life.	Changing the topic.	Telling him not to worry about others.	Not raise the subject of his friends doing well in their careers and lives. Distract Jim and lead him to a different topic of conversation that he enjoys when he talks about his friends doing well.

Your turn

Think of an example of when the person has become aggressive.

What happened?	What have I tried before?		What will I do in the future?
	What worked?	What didn't work?	

CHAPTER 17

Dealing with Problems Associated with Tobacco, Alcohol and Drug Use

Problems associated with tobacco, alcohol and drug use

Before Dominic had schizophrenia, I didn't worry too much when he was drunk. But now it's a different story. I can see how drinking alcohol affects his illness, and he smokes a lot more than he used to. I wish he didn't hang around with that group of friends who drink and smoke all of the time.

Just like the general community, many people with schizophrenia use licit (legal) drugs (such as tobacco and alcohol), whereas use of illicit substances (drugs that are illegal, such as cannabis, heroin and methamphetamine) is less common (and type of use can vary by country). The most frequently used drugs by people with schizophrenia (in descending order) are:

1. Tobacco: classified as a drug because it contains nicotine. Cigarette smoking is much more common in people with schizophrenia (over 60%) than in the general population (approximately 13% in Australia). Nicotine is the main chemical in tobacco; however, tobacco contains many other harmful chemicals. Nicotine is an extremely addictive drug. Long-term use of tobacco has serious adverse effects on a person's health; for example, it can cause cancer, heart disease, stroke, chronic lung disease and reduced life expectancy. In fact, people with schizophrenia have a mortality rate three times higher than people in the general population, and this is mostly due the harms associated with cigarette smoking. Furthermore, people with schizophrenia who smoke heavily may require a higher dose of antipsychotic medication to treat their illness than non-smokers.

2. Alcohol (beer, wine, spirits or premixed drinks): a depressant substance that slows down the speed of messages traveling between the brain and the body. Drinking heavily can worsen a person's mood and anxiety, and can also increase the likelihood of making poor decisions. Heavy alcohol intake can also worsen positive symptoms (increasing the risk of relapse) of schizophrenia.

3. Cannabis (marijuana): a depressant drug that slows down the speed of messages traveling between the brain and the body and can also have a hallucinogenic effect. Regular use can worsen positive symptoms (increasing the risk of relapse) and affect mood and motivation.

4. Amphetamines: stimulant drugs that increase the speed of messages traveling between the brain and the body. Frequent use can lead to rapidly changing moods (being elevated, irritable or depressed) and anxiety, as well as worsening positive symptoms (increasing the risk of relapse and aggressive behavior). While amphetamines can be prescribed legally by a doctor as a medication for certain conditions, illicit amphetamines are available in three forms:

    a. Speed: usually available in powder form.

    b. Base: available as an oily, sticky or waxy paste.

    c. Ice (crystal methamphetamine): available as a crystal or crystalline powder. Ice is a stronger form of methamphetamine, and is commonly called "crystal meth," "glass" or "shabu."

The following drugs are less commonly used by people with schizophrenia:

- Opioids: depressant drugs that slow down the speed of messages traveling between the brain and the body. They are typically prescribed by a doctor to relieve severe pain. They are available as prescription medications (e.g. morphine, oxycodone, codeine) or as the street drug heroin. Most of the harms associated with opioid use are a consequence of injecting the drug (such as increasing the chance of becoming infected with the viruses hepatitis B and C) as well as the risk of overdose.

- Cocaine (coke, crack, Charlie, nose candy, sugar block): a stimulant drug that is similar in effect to the amphetamines. There are three illicit forms of the drug:

    - Cocaine hydrochloride: a white powder that is frequently mixed or "cut" with other substances.

- Freebase: a white powder that is purer than cocaine hydrochloride.

- Crack: a crystal form that varies in color (white, cream, transparent, pink or yellow hue) and may contain impurities.

According to research, people with schizophrenia are more likely to develop a substance use problem than members of the general public. Even if the person you are supporting does not regularly use tobacco, alcohol or drugs, or only takes these substances occasionally, it is important to be aware of their harmful effect on the person's treatment, and to know how to deal with problems should they arise.

Some drugs interfere with prescribed medications. Alcohol in small amounts may be fine with some medications. However, for others, it may directly interfere with the effectiveness of the medication. Similarly, heavy cigarette smoking increases the need for higher doses of antipsychotic medication as it increases the body's ability to break down these medications more quickly. However, if the person reduces the amount they smoke or quits smoking, they may need to reduce their medication dose. You can discuss recommendations regarding the interaction between tobacco, alcohol and drug use and the person's prescribed medications with your health professional.

Multiple treatments are available to help someone who has developed problems related to their drug use. Options include specific psychological therapies, including cognitive behavior therapy. If the person has become addicted to the drug and experiences severe withdrawal symptoms when they stop using it, they may require admission to hospital to help them detoxify from the drug. There are also several medications available to help people who have developed addiction to certain drugs (such as methadone or buprenorphine for addiction to opiate drugs, and naltrexone and acamprosate for addiction to alcohol); you can talk to your health professional for further information. Peer support groups, such as Alcoholics Anonymous and Narcotics Anonymous, provide important support for people trying to cease using, although you may need to help the person find a meeting that provides particular support for people who also have a mental illness.

Most countries have services dedicated to supporting people with alcohol and drug problems, as it is a common issue in the general population. These services may provide information, support, counseling or group therapy. There are also many services accessible online via the Internet, and these often also provide support to family members. There are also family support groups available in most areas, including those run by services as well as Al-Anon, and these provide an important resource for families to learn from the experiences of other families and share some of the challenges they face.

Dual diagnosis

Dual diagnosis is a term that is commonly used to refer to people who are diagnosed with a mental health disorder and a substance use problem. Many people with problems related to their alcohol and drug use experience mental health problems, and these problems occur at higher rates than in the general community. Often it is hard to know which came first: perhaps the mental illness led the person to use drugs to help cope with unpleasant emotions, or the illness developed after they began using drugs. For example, smoking cannabis heavily or taking methamphetamines can trigger a psychotic episode; however, substance use may increase as part of the prodromal (first) phase of schizophrenia.

Often, health services may treat mental health problems and substance use problems separately. In these cases, the person with schizophrenia and alcohol and drug problems may be referred to more than one service to receive treatment. This may mean appointments to see different health professionals, and one service may not communicate well with another.

It is important for you and the person to keep track of what each service says or recommends. One way to address this problem is to be organized. This may involve:

- Keeping a diary of when appointments occur, with whom, at which service, and what the professionals say and/or prescribe.

- Maintaining good relationships with the health professionals of each service.

- Maintaining a list of contact names, addresses and telephone numbers of each service.

- Discussing with each health professional the best way to organize or manage going to more than one service, or try to find a service where the mental health and substance use issues are treated together.

Harmful effects of regular substance use

Alcohol or drug use (and to a lesser extent, cigarette smoking) can interfere with a person's treatment plan, even if they are only taken rarely. Harmful effects include:

- Worsening mood, such as feeling down, depressed and low.

- Increasing irritability.

- Worsening positive symptoms, such as hallucinations or delusions.

- Increasing feelings of paranoia or anxiety.

Overall, people with schizophrenia who use substances regularly are at a greater risk of:

- Developing addiction to the substance (having a psychological need to use the drug despite harmful consequences). Symptoms of addiction include:

  - Craving—a strong urge to use the substance.

  - Difficulty in controlling use of the substance.

  - Spending a great deal of time trying to obtain the substance.

  - Taking larger amounts of the substance or using over a longer period of time than intended.

  - Repeated unsuccessful attempts to reduce the level of substance use.

  - Continuing to use drugs despite being aware of the psychological or physical problems associated with continued use.

- Becoming physically dependent on the substance (i.e. the body becomes used to the drug and develops responses to minimize its effects). Symptoms include:

  - Tolerance—the need to greatly increase the amount of the substance used to experience the desired effect.

  - Withdrawal syndrome—symptoms that occur when the person stops using the drug after prolonged heavy use. Withdrawal symptoms vary depending on the drug used but are typically the opposite to what is experienced when the drug is taken (for example, anxiety, restlessness, sweating, insomnia, low mood, irritability, lethargy, nausea). Withdrawal is a very stressful experience and needs to be managed in consultation with your health professional. This is important as a severe withdrawal syndrome can precipitate a psychotic relapse.

- Experiencing problems with friends and family, at work or school, or with the law.

- Experiencing financial problems (substances are expensive).

- Relapse.

- Being admitted to hospital.

- Having a prolonged recovery time.

- Experiencing longer-lasting psychotic symptoms.

- Displaying aggressive behavior.

- Worsening their ability to function on a day-to-day basis.

- Having other mental health problems, such as depression or anxiety.

- Having poor health overall or serious health problems, for example lung cancer (from smoking cigarettes) or liver disease (from drinking alcohol).

Why substance use occurs

If possible, talk with the person to try to work out why they are using substances. People use or take substances for a variety of reasons, such as to feel pleasure or get a "high," lessen stress or boredom, help feel relaxed or to sleep, cope with low moods, to fit in with their friends (if they use substances), or out of habit or routine. A person may also use or take substances because they feel socially isolated or, alternatively, to socialize with other people who do, or they feel it helps them socialize with other people (because it helps them deal with their anxiety in social settings).

From the carer's perspective, it is difficult to understand why the person you are supporting drinks, smokes cigarettes or takes drugs when it has a harmful effect on them.

You, your family and friends may have feelings of frustration, anxiety, anger, helplessness or despair at the situation. These are all common emotions felt by those who have a family member with schizophrenia who regularly uses substances.

To help all of you cope better with the situation, you can seek assistance from support services. The health professional should be able to put you in contact with the appropriate services or support groups. Feel free to talk to them about the situation, too.

Helping the person deal with their substance use

Recovery from regular substance use is a gradual process. It involves the person developing awareness of their problem (see the section on impaired awareness, in Chapter 6), having motivation to make a change, and then gaining the skills and support for changing their behavior and developing a healthier lifestyle.

Living with someone with regular substance use and a mental illness can be difficult. As a carer, you may feel anxious, stressed, fearful for the future and sometimes guilty. You also may feel the need to take control of the person's substance use in order to be supportive. However, it is preferable if you can support the person to take responsibility to deal with their substance use. Try to avoid focusing on the person's shortcomings as this just increases conflict between you both. Instead, try to focus on their achievements, such as praising them for cutting down on or not using substances, or adopting a healthier lifestyle.

The following tips are suggestions for how to support the person, to enable them to make a change to their substance use.

Ways in which you, family and friends can support the person

- Praise their achievements, no matter how small; avoid any temptation to engage in criticism.

- Help them to educate themselves about the harmful effects of substance use on their disorder and overall health.

- Help them identify the benefits and costs of their substance use. For example, ask them to write down what the positive things about using are (e.g. to feel relaxed, to help socialize, to deal with boredom), as well as the harmful things (e.g. impact on mood, positive symptoms, relationships and finances).

- Talk openly with them about the problem. Express your concerns and try to understand their perspective.

- Explore other ways the person may deal with common reasons they may be using substances (e.g. addressing boredom, social anxiety, getting to sleep, relaxing).

- Encourage them to seek help for their problem, such as by attending self-help groups, treatment services or counseling sessions.

- Help them to make a plan of how to reduce or avoid taking harmful substances.

- Encourage them to tell family and friends not to offer them any substances and explain why they should avoid using substances, such as the potentially harmful effects on their psychotic disorder.

- Help to keep substances that they have problems with away from them. Try to avoid keeping cigarettes, alcohol or drugs at home.

- Try to set a good example yourself by not engaging in regular substance use.

- Encourage them to say "no" to offers of alcohol or drugs.

- Encourage them to think of alternative ways to socialize or gain enjoyment without using drugs, such as beginning a hobby or joining a support group.

- Gently remind them of the benefits of not using substances, such as improved recovery and better health.

- Try to build their self-esteem and help them feel better about themselves.

- Encourage them to participate in enjoyable activities that provide them with a sense of achievement.

- Emphasize their positive achievements, such as congratulating them when treatment guidelines have been followed.

- Be patient with their progress. Treating substance use problems can take time.

- Agree on a set of house rules. For example, not smoking cigarettes or taking alcohol or drugs in the house.

Things you, family and friends should try to avoid doing

- Threaten the person if substance use occurs, such as saying you will call the police or the health professional.

- Encourage substance use.

- Glamorize occasions when substances have been used. For example, don't say, "We all got really drunk last night…it was great."

- Place them in a situation where alcohol or drugs are easily available, such as bringing them to a party where everyone will be drinking alcohol.

- Isolate, criticize or be angry with them when they use substances.

Harm minimization

Despite the person's and your best efforts, they may continue to use substances, and it is therefore helpful to try to encourage the person to consider ways to minimize harm associated with their use to themselves and others.

Harm minimization is a common approach that health professionals use to support the person to minimize the harmful consequences associated with their alcohol and drug use. This is not about going "soft," "not taking drugs seriously" or condoning drug use, but about identifying the harmful effects for individuals, those around them and the community, and implementing strategies to reduce any potential harm.

These are some common ways the person can reduce the amount of harm to themselves and others:

- Trying to reduce the number of cigarettes smoked and amount of alcohol consumed or drugs taken.

- Avoiding driving or operating machinery when under the influence of alcohol or drugs.

- Opting for low-alcohol drinks.

- Opting for low-nicotine cigarettes.

- Avoiding taking alcohol or drugs alone or with people they don't trust.

- Avoiding taking drugs or alcohol in unsafe environments (like a pub or bar with a reputation of violence, or an abandoned warehouse).

- Avoiding mixing drugs or taking alcohol and drugs together.

- Using condoms and keeping them close by.

- If the person is injecting drugs (a less common situation in people with schizophrenia):

    - Avoiding sharing syringes or needles.

    - Disposing of syringes and needles safely.

    - Getting tested regularly for known diseases.

    - Ensuring vaccinations (immunizations) are up to date.

KEY POINTS TO REMEMBER

- It is important to be aware of how tobacco, alcohol and drugs can have harmful effects on the person's health and treatment, and how to deal with common problems that can arise.

- Tobacco smoking is very common among people with schizophrenia and contributes to early death and a range of physical illnesses.

- The most common types of substances used by people with schizophrenia are alcohol and the illicit drugs cannabis and amphetamines.

- People with schizophrenia who use substances are at a greater risk of relapse and other health and social problems.

- For the carer, family and friends it is difficult to come to terms with seeing the person use substances if it is clear that such use is affecting their schizophrenia and causing additional health problems. It is helpful to seek assistance from support services and speak to a health professional regarding advice about how to best support the person around their substance use.

- Recovery from substance use can be a gradual process. You can support the person if they have problems with their substance use by:

  - Talking openly with them about their problem, effects on their mental and physical wellbeing, and encouraging them to seek help.

  - Emphasizing their positive achievements and being patient with their progress.

  - Encouraging them to consider ways to minimize harm to themselves and others.

  - Supporting them to build their self-esteem and coping, and encouraging them to feel better about themselves.

  - Overcoming boredom by supporting them to achieve a sense of purpose and fulfillment in life.

ACTIVITY: Problem-solving

This activity is an opportunity to practice solving problems related to the topic "Dealing with problems associated with tobacco, alcohol and drug use." First, remind yourself of the summary of the ADAPT 5-step method of effective problem-solving (see Chapter 4).

A problem has been worked out using the five steps of the ADAPT method:

Situation: Yuan is Lee's mother and carer. Lee is being treated for schizophrenia and there are concerns about his heavy drinking.

Problem: When Lee sees his friends drink alcohol, he is tempted to drink too, and often drinks more than he says he intends to. When he comes home, he is irritable and verbally aggressive towards family members.

ATTITUDE

Adopt a positive, optimistic attitude.

Yuan believes that if she gives Lee support and encouragement he will not feel tempted to drink alcohol when he is with his friends.

DEFINE

Define the problem. State the facts, identify obstacles and specify a goal.

Lee enjoys seeing his friends, but all of them drink alcohol. He goes out to see his friends once a week usually at a place where alcohol is available. Lee tries to consume only soft drinks, but his friends often offer to buy him beer. His friends know he is ill and that he should not drink too much alcohol, but they do not seem to understand why he cannot control his drinking.

ALTERNATIVES

Generate a list of different alternatives for overcoming the problem and achieving a goal.

1. *Yuan encourages Lee to explain to his friends about his illness, why it is important that he does not drink alcohol and asks them not to offer him alcohol.*

2. *Yuan encourages Lee to be with his friends at venues where no alcohol is served, such as the movie theater or an alcohol-free café.*

3. *Yuan helps Lee think of ways to say no to his friends when they offer him alcohol.*

4. *Yuan encourages Lee not to see his friends and to get new friends who do not drink.*

PREDICT

Predict the helpful and unhelpful consequences for each alternative. Choose the best one to achieve your goal that minimizes costs and maximizes benefits.

Alternatives	Helpful consequences	Unhelpful consequences
Alternative 1	Lee can still see his friends. Lee's friends understand properly why he cannot drink alcohol and stop offering him alcohol. Lee feels less pressure to drink alcohol and is less tempted to drink any.	Lee's friends may still offer him alcohol and he may still be tempted to drink.
Alternative 2	Lee can still see his friends. Lee does not feel any pressure to drink alcohol and he is not tempted to drink.	Lee may not be able to see his friends as much as before because they may want to go to places that serve alcohol.
Alternative 3	Lee still gets to see his friends. Lee strengthens his ability to not drink alcohol.	Lee's friends may still offer him alcohol and he still may be tempted to drink.
Alternative 4	Lee does not feel any pressure to drink alcohol and he is not tempted to drink. Lee enjoys making new friends.	Lee may have difficulties finding new friends, and it may take a long time, so he may not get to go out or socialize as much. Lee enjoys seeing his original friends.

Best alternative: *Yuan chooses to try alternatives 1, 2 and 3 because she knows Lee enjoys being with his friends.*

TRY OUT

Try out the solution in "real life." See if it works, and evaluate it.

Try out: *Yuan tried out alternatives 1, 2 and 3. The next time Lee met his friends at the cinema, he explained to them why he can't drink and asked them not to offer him any drinks. His friends all seemed to care and said they would help. But some of them still wanted to meet at venues that served alcohol. Two weeks later, they all met at the pub and none of Lee's friends offered him any alcohol.*

Problem solved: *Yes, in the short term, as Lee is not drinking alcohol when he is with his friends.*

Think of a problem you are experiencing with the person you are supporting related to the topic "Dealing with problems associated with tobacco, alcohol and drug use." First, briefly describe the situation and the problem, then complete the blank ADAPT table below.

Situation:

_____

_____

_____

Problem:

_____

_____

_____

ATTITUDE **Adopt a positive, optimistic attitude.**

⬇

DEFINE **Define the problem. State the facts, identify obstacles and specify a goal.**

⬇

ALTERNATIVES **Generate a list of different alternatives for overcoming the problem and achieving a goal.**

PREDICT

Predict the helpful and unhelpful consequences for each
alternative. Choose the best one to achieve your goal
that minimizes costs and maximizes benefits.

Alternatives	Helpful consequences	Unhelpful consequences

Best alternative:

TRY OUT

Try out the solution in "real life." See if it works, and evaluate it.

Try out:

Problem solved:

CHAPTER 18

Dealing with Suicide and Self-Harm

Suicide

It is devastating to think someone close to you may consider attempting suicide. You may think the person you are supporting would never think of such a thing, but it is better to be prepared for all circumstances. Suicide is the biggest cause of premature death among people with schizophrenia. The best way to minimize the risk of suicide is by supporting the person to maintain good mental wellbeing. This in itself is a challenge for the person, so it is helpful to develop a plan of what to do when you recognize the warning signs of suicide.

There are many forms of support available to help you look after someone who is suicidal. Help is available from the health professional, community services, hospitals, GPs, counselors, psychiatrists and services set up specifically for suicide prevention. You may also want to attend a mental health first aid course to learn more about dealing with someone who is suicidal.

The main risk periods for suicide for the person are during the acute phase of schizophrenia and during setbacks in the recovery phase. Also, people who have attempted suicide in the past are at a higher risk of suicidal behavior in the future.

To minimize the risk of suicide, if possible, it is helpful if you and others close to the person are aware of and are able to watch out for warning signs in their behavior and immediately alert health professionals.

Please feel assured that there are people who want to help you support the person and who are willing to listen.

Depression and suicide

Depression occurs more often in people with schizophrenia than in the general population. Depression is a major risk factor for suicide, especially in men. However, while depression is a contributing factor in most suicides, the person does not have to be depressed to attempt or complete suicide. The risk of suicide is greater when the person is experiencing depression and schizophrenia.

Please refer to Chapter 11 for information on how to deal with depression.

Warning signs of suicide

It is important to be aware of the warning signs of suicide when supporting a person with schizophrenia. The warning signs include, but are not limited to:

- Being preoccupied with death: talking about death a lot, or talking about suicide.

- A marked change in the person's behavior: sudden changes in how the person relates to others, withdrawing from friends or family, sudden happiness after a lengthy period of depression, or increased use of drugs or alcohol.

- Depression: feelings of hopelessness and helplessness; for example, feeling useless, as if there is no future for them.

- Making statements suggesting suicide, such as "I wish I was dead," "You won't have to worry about me soon," "Maybe I will disappear for good" or "I'd like to go to sleep and never wake up."

- Threatening to hurt or kill themselves.

- Looking for ways to kill themselves, such as seeking access to medications or weapons.

- Making final arrangements, such as preparing a will, writing a letter, giving away personal belongings, taking out life insurance or saying "goodbye."

- Lack of self-concern: not worrying about getting hurt, or lack of interest in health in general, or eating or sleeping.

- Engaging in reckless or risky behavior, without considering the consequences.

- Self-harm: deliberately inflicting self-injury, for instance bruising themselves or cutting their wrists or arms.

- Increasing alcohol or drug use.

- Increasing agitation during the acute phase of the disorder.

The person may show a combination of warning signs of suicide, or only one sign.

Responding to the warning signs

Many people do not know what to do when they recognize the warning signs of suicide in the person they are supporting. They may be afraid they will make the situation worse by trying to help, talking with them about it or drawing attention to it. This is not the case. Asking them about their suicidal thoughts will give them the opportunity to talk about their problems, and if you approach the person with sensitivity and empathy, you are showing that you care.

When talking with the person, try to stay calm and ask how they feel. Listen to what they say and try to imagine what it feels like to experience what they are going through. Their problems may seem more manageable after they have been discussed with someone.

Suggestions that may help you recognize the warning signs

- Try not to overreact or have an emotional outburst. If you think you may have difficulty discussing suicide with them, ask someone else to talk to them.

- Listen to their feelings, but point out that help is available and that they are not alone.

- Show appreciation for their feelings and the fact that you have been confided in.

- Be supportive, but not overprotective.

- Be polite and respectful; try to avoid telling them what they should and should not do.

- Tell them that you care, want to help and will always be there to give them support.

- Make sure they are around other people who are supportive and non-judgemental.

- Encourage involvement in pleasant, simple activities, if possible.

- Ask them to promise to talk to you or the health professional, or telephone a crisis support and suicide prevention helpline when thoughts of suicide reoccur.

Things to try to avoid doing when you recognize the warning signs

- Discuss with the person whether suicide is right or wrong. For example, avoid bringing up spiritual or religious views about suicide.

- Joke, be sarcastic or laugh about the situation.

- Argue with them.

- Suggest a quick-fix solution, such as saying, "Why don't you have a sleep? I'm sure you will feel better tomorrow."

- Tell them to "pull themselves together" or "get over it."

- Use the term "commit" suicide. It gives the impression that suicide is a sin or a crime (the correct term to use is to "complete" suicide). Likewise, avoid using the term "failed" suicide attempt or "unsuccessful" suicide attempt, as they imply that death would have been a positive outcome.

- Keep it a secret.

- Ignore the signs and put off telling the health professional.

How to tell if the situation is serious

To determine whether someone has definite intentions to take their life or whether they are having less serious suicidal thoughts (for example, if they are saying "What's the point of going on?"), you can ask if they feel suicidal. You might ask any of the following questions:

- Are you having thoughts about suicide?

- Are you thinking about killing yourself?

- Do you want to hurt yourself?

If they indicate *they have not been thinking about suicide*, you could still talk with them about how they are feeling and if they are experiencing any problems. Let them know you will support them through any difficulties and suggest they get in contact with the health professional. It is still worthwhile that they telephone a crisis support and suicide prevention helpline, and for you to speak with the health professional, if possible, about how they are feeling.

If they say *they have been feeling suicidal*, you could ask more questions, such as:

- Have you decided how you would kill yourself?

- Have you decided when you would do it?

- Have you taken steps to secure things you would need to carry it out?

You will also need to ascertain if they have been drinking alcohol or taking drugs, as this can make them more susceptible to acting rashly or impulsively.

A higher level of planning indicates a more serious risk. However, the absence of a plan does not mean they are safe. All thoughts of suicide must be taken seriously. Once you recognize that the risk of suicide is present, you must take immediate action to keep the person safe.

Immediate and direct steps to take when you think there is a risk of suicide

- Ensure the person is safe and that you and others are safe.

- Immediately contact the emergency services or any mental health emergency numbers you may have been given. Make sure you keep emergency contact telephone numbers nearby at home or on your mobile phone (cell phone) when you are away from home.

- Put your emergency plan into place. The emergency plan should include:

  - Removing people or things that may cause stress or difficulties, and removing the person from stressful or difficult situations.

  - Making sure there is nothing nearby that the person can use to inflict self-harm. If the person has a weapon or is behaving aggressively towards you, seek assistance from the police or authorities to protect yourself and others.

  - Ensuring drugs and alcohol are inaccessible.

  - Making sure someone stays with the person until help arrives, if it is safe to do so.

It is also important to discuss with the health professional beforehand what to do in case the person has suicidal thoughts or is attempting suicide.

In some situations, the person may refuse help. While it is essential you get help, it does not guarantee help will be accepted or appreciated. Thoughts of suicide do not disappear easily, but may persist over a long period. You will need as much help from others as possible as the person may need 24-hour attention. This is not a responsibility that you should carry by yourself.

Treating suicidal behavior requires professional help. The health professional may hospitalize the person if they are presenting a risk to themselves or others, and/or they may propose a different treatment plan.

What should you do if the person asks you to promise not to tell anyone about their suicide plan? Avoid agreeing to keep a suicide plan a secret. While respecting the person's right to privacy, try to involve them in decisions about who else should be informed about their plan.

Self-harm

Self-harm is when people deliberately do physical damage to their body. They intentionally and repeatedly cause self-harm, and may do this in a number of ways, such as cutting, scratching, bruising or burning themselves, taking a drug overdose or poisonous substances, or swallowing things. There are also less obvious ways of self-harm, which you may not think of, such as staying in an abusive relationship, or being addicted to drugs or alcohol.

It is generally agreed that people who self-harm often do not intend to die because of their actions, although death may occur. As a result, the risk of suicide and accidental death is far greater for those who self-harm. Self-harm is a complicated problem and difficult to deal with, and most people suffer with significant psychological distress.

People may engage in self-harm for many reasons, such as to manage painful feelings, punish themselves or communicate with others. They may see self-harm as the main strategy for coping with problems, and self-harm over a long period of time. For these people it can be very difficult to break the habit of self-harming.

It is not always easy to tell the difference between non-suicidal self-harm and a suicide attempt. Ask the person directly if they are suicidal, as in the information above.

People diagnosed with schizophrenia may be at risk of harming themselves in the acute phase of the disorder and during difficulties and setbacks in the recovery phase. Many people with schizophrenia who continue to self-harm have an additional mental health problem, such as depression or a personality disorder.

Warning signs of self-harm

A person who is self-harming may have frequent unexplained injuries, try to hide that they are injured or may reveal that they have been harming themselves. Other people may hide their injuries, making it difficult to detect what they have been doing.

Warning signs of self-harm include, but are not limited to:

- Unexplained injuries, such as scratches, cuts, bruises, burns, bite marks or fractured bones.

- Drug or alcohol use.

- Unexplained physical complaints, such as headaches or stomach pains.

- Wearing clothes that cover up arms and legs, for example in hot weather, and avoiding situations where they have to expose their arms or legs, such as swimming.

Take all self-harm behavior seriously, no matter how trivial the injury or the intention behind it.

Responding to self-harm

Help the person seek medical attention when their injuries are serious, for example if a wound needs stitches or you suspect a broken bone. If the person has taken an overdose, call the emergency service straight away.

Similar to responding to the situation when a person has attempted suicide, it can also be confronting dealing with the situation where a person is self-harming. If you suspect the person is doing so or contemplating it, you could try to talk to them about it, as well as contact the health professional.

Most importantly, when attempting to talk to the person about the situation, try to stay calm and avoid overreacting or becoming angry or frustrated. Speak clearly with them about how you are there to help, support and listen to them. However, it may be difficult for the person to talk about why they are self-harming. Encourage them to speak to the health professional or other trustworthy specialist if they are reluctant to talk to you.

You can encourage the person to think of other ways to cope with their problems instead of self-harming. You can help them make a plan about what they could do when they are distressed and feel like self-harming. This could include positive coping strategies such as talking with someone about their problems, or engaging in a relaxing or enjoyable activity.

As in the case of suicide, do not promise to keep the person's self-harming behavior a secret. Make them aware that you cannot do this. If you are going to speak to someone about the situation—for example, the health professional—tell the person that you will be doing so beforehand.

Keep in mind that self-harming is a complicated problem that requires a lot of support from health professionals and those surrounding the person. Do not try to deal with it by yourself. Professional help is needed and a new treatment plan needs to be put in place to help the person overcome this behavior.

KEY POINTS TO REMEMBER

- Suicide is the largest cause of premature death of people with schizophrenia. The risk of suicide is greater when the person is experiencing depression and schizophrenia, and if the person has attempted suicide in the past.

- Learn about the warning signs of suicide, which include a person being preoccupied with death or making statements suggesting suicide or depression, or threatening to hurt or kill themselves.

- Act quickly and directly when you think there is a threat of suicide. Ensure the person, you or others are safe, and contact emergency services. Treating suicidal behavior requires professional help.

- Self-harm is when people deliberately do physical damage to their body. They intentionally and repeatedly hurt themselves.

- Take all self-harm behavior seriously, no matter how trivial the injury or the intention behind it. Self-harm is a complicated problem that requires a lot of support from health professionals and those surrounding the person.

- When you attempt to talk to the person about the situation, try to stay calm and not overreact or become angry or frustrated. Speak clearly with them about how you are there to help, support and listen to them.

CHAPTER 19

The Future

As you have come to the end of *The Carer's Guide to Schizophrenia: A Concise, Problem-Solving Resource for Family and Friends*, you may ask yourself:

- What happens next?

- Will the person recover completely?

- What if they do not recover completely; what can I do then?

Schizophrenia is like any other medical illness in that it is treatable. Most people make a good recovery and lead satisfying and productive lives, but need maintenance treatment. The pattern of recovery varies from person to person. Some people recover quickly with very little treatment. Others need support over a longer period.

As discussed earlier in the book, recovery can mean different things to different people. "Clinical recovery" can be described as when the person stops experiencing the symptoms of schizophrenia. "Realistic recovery" can be described as when the person feels able to manage their symptoms, accepts their situation, is working towards their goals and has hope for the future.

Working towards realistic recovery will better equip the person to manage their disorder, feel good about themselves and be able to deal better with relapse.

To recap, here are some recovery principles you can support the person in working towards:

- Acceptance: accepting they have schizophrenia and its symptoms.

- Identity: supporting them to reclaim their identity and not feel "labeled" by their disorder or that it should dominate their life.

- Empowerment and independence: supporting them to take control of their life.

- Coping and self-management: supporting them to develop healthy techniques to self-manage and cope with the disorder.

- Meaning and sense of purpose: encouraging and supporting them to find and do what is important to them and that they enjoy, and to continue to pursue their dreams and goals.

- Praise: praising them for their achievements, no matter how small. Avoiding the temptation to criticize them.

- Confidence: supporting them to rebuild their self-confidence and self-esteem.

- Social connection: encouraging them to maintain relationships with family and friends and to build new relationships with others.

- Hope: encouraging them to accept that there is hope for recovery and to have a good quality of life.

The person's recovery

Unfortunately, it is difficult to forecast what the person's recovery will be like as each case is different. Three scenarios are described below to give you a guide as to what may occur in the future. However, do not assume that any of these situations will definitely happen.

Complete recovery with no relapse

Kathleen's mother was her main carer and they worked together to help Kathleen recover. Kathleen experienced some setbacks in the recovery phase, as she took some drugs when she knew she shouldn't have. This prolonged her recovery, but she swore that she wouldn't do it again, and managed to make a complete recovery. She has not experienced another episode of schizophrenia.

Complete recovery, but future relapses

Ari's father was his main carer and was very supportive of Ari following his treatment. Ari found it difficult to manage his mood swings despite the treatment plan. He made a complete recovery but had an episode of schizophrenia six months later. This time Ari and his father knew what to expect and what they needed to do to help Ari manage his mood swings. They were able to get the right support from services.

Incomplete recovery and future relapses

Caitlin's auntie is her main carer and supported Caitlin throughout her treatment at the mental health service. Caitlin and her auntie worked together and Caitlin followed the treatment plan, but she did not manage to recover completely. She has had two more episodes of schizophrenia since she left the mental health service. She still receives treatment in the form of antipsychotic medication and cognitive behavioral therapy, and attends a self-help group for people with schizophrenia.

Even when a person is in the recovery phase, it is important that they continue to monitor their disorder and use the self-management techniques they have learnt such as meditation, mindfulness or self-help groups.

A final word

By now you will have experienced more of what it is like to be a carer of a person with schizophrenia than you did when you began this book. You may still find it overwhelming as you read through the book and deal with things in real life, or you may feel you are able to cope better. Perhaps you and the person have grown closer or perhaps you have a different relationship than you had before.

In your role you will become extremely knowledgeable in understanding what schizophrenia is, and will become highly experienced in accessing, communicating with and getting support from mental health services. These are all valid and important skills that will help the person throughout their disorder and beyond. Do not think of yourself as "just a carer"; your role is essential and highly important.

We hope that *The Carer's Guide to Schizophrenia: A Concise, Problem-Solving Resource for Family and Friends* helps you in some ways and strengthens your confidence to continue in your support role. There are a few general tips that we would like to leave you with:

- Look after yourself.

- As far as possible, be open and collaborate with the person with schizophrenia.

- Get help: don't try to do things by yourself, use available support services.

- Talk to others: tell them how you are feeling and coping.

- Take a break when things get too much to bear.

- Appreciate yourself: you are doing an important and demanding job.

- Reward yourself: remember to do things you enjoy.

- Be optimistic and hopeful for the future.

Internet Contacts for Carers, Family and Friends

Australia
Carer Gateway
An Australian Government initiative for carers; provides practical information and advice, and facilitates access to services and support. Also provides free telephone counseling services and coaching, and enables carers to connect with other carers through a community forum.

www.carergateway.gov.au

Carers Australia
Provides a range of carer services and information resources.

www.carersaustralia.com.au

Children of Parents with a Mental Illness (COPMI)
National online site providing information and resources for parents, family, friends and young people, including young carers whose parents have mental illness.

www.copmi.net.au

Grow
Community-based organization that provides information on mental illness and specializes in providing support meetings for people with mental illness and their families.

www.grow.org.au

Hearing Voices Network Australia

A community of voice hearers, professionals and families, who work toward recovery, acceptance and inclusion.

www.hearing-voices.org

Mental Health Carers Australia

A group of mental health carer organizations, with representation throughout Australia.

www.mentalhealthcarersaustralia.org.au

Mental Health First Aid (MHFA) Australia

Provides mental health training and research. Provides helpful guides for how to deal with particular mental health problems. Currently, over 25 countries have licensed and adapted the MHFA Australia program for their own settings, and more than three million people worldwide have been trained in MHFA skills.

www.mhfa.com.au

Mental Illness Fellowship of Australia

A group of mental illness organizations with representation throughout Australia.

www.mifa.org.au

Neuroscience Research Australia (NeuRA)

National medical research center dedicated to brain and nervous system research. Provides current information and research on schizophrenia and other mental disorders.

www.neura.edu.au

One Door Mental Health

Community-based organization committed to creating a world where people with mental illness, their families and carers are valued and treated as equals. Formerly known as Schizophrenia Fellowship of NSW.

www.onedoor.org.au

PeerZone Australia

A peer-developed and peer-led resource that provides workshops, training and consultancy to support people with lived experience of mental distress or addiction to develop their roles in helping others. Operates in several countries (Australia, Canada, New Zealand, USA).

www.peerzone.info

ReachOut
Australia's online youth mental health service.

www.au.reachout.com

Sane Australia
Provides information, a helpline and separate online forums for carers and people with mental disorders.

www.sane.org

Skylight Mental Health
Aims to reduce discrimination and the stigma of mental illness. Provides support and information for people with mental illness and for their family and friends. Also builds community awareness and advocates for improved mental health policies and services.

www.skylight.org.au

Wellways
A not-for-profit mental health and disability support organization. Provides a wide range of services for people with mental health issues or disability, as well as family, friends and carers.

www.wellways.org

Young Carers Network
A national online network which provides information on support services, resources and sharing of personal experiences for children and young people up to 25 years old who support family with mental or physical health issues or disability.

https://youngcarersnetwork.com.au

Canada
AMI-Quebec
A not-for-profit organization which enables families to cope with the effects of mental illness in a family member. Provides a comprehensive range of

programs and activities to support, educate, guide and advocate for carers. Specific programs include workshops, support groups, counseling, online learning, events, public awareness presentations and hospital-based family peer support.

www.amiquebec.org

Canadian Clinical Community
Alliance of carer organizations throughout Canada with links to local carer organizations.

https://mcconnellfoundation.ca/www.ccc-ccan.ca

Canadian Mental Health Association
Most extensive national organization in Canada; has branches across the country that provide mental health information, support (including peer support) and services.

www.cmha.ca

Caregivers Nova Scotia
Provides information, workshops and peer support groups for carers, and the means to get in contact with local services in Nova Scotia.

www.caregiversns.org

Carers Canada
National caregiver coalition of diverse federal and provincial organizations that join with carers, providers, policy makers and other stakeholders to effect positive change for carers.

www.carerscanada.ca

Mental Health Commission of Canada
National organization leading the development and dissemination of innovative programs and tools to support the mental health and wellness of Canadians, and the implementation of sound public mental health policy. Key resources:

- National Guidelines for a Comprehensive Service System to Support Family Caregivers of Adults with Mental Health Problems and Illnesses (www.mentalhealthcommission.ca/sites/default/files/Caregiving_MHCC_Family_Caregivers_Guidelines_ENG_0.pdf).

- Taking Caregiver Guidelines Off the Shelf—Mobilization Toolkit (www.mentalhealthcommission.ca/sites/default/files/Getting% 252520Started%252520-%252520Background%252520on%252520 the%252520Issue%252520_0_0.pdf).

www.mentalhealthcommission.ca/English

Mental Health First Aid (MHFA) Canada

Provides mental health training and research. Provides helpful guides for how to deal with particular mental health problems. Currently, over 25 countries have licensed and adapted the MHFA Australia program for their own settings, and more than three million people worldwide have been trained in MHFA skills.

www.mhfa.ca

Mental Illness Caregivers Association of Canada

National organization supporting caregivers and their members to manage the effects of serious and persistent mental illness and/or addictions through education, guidance and support, including how to navigate the mental health and/or addiction systems.

www.micaontario.com

Mindyourmind

A mental health online resource for young people that provides information and programs to support young people with mental illness.

www.mindyourmind.ca

National Alliance on Mental Illness

A not-for-profit organization based in Ontario. Offers programs for people with mental illness and their family and friends who reside in Ontario and in Dorval, Quebec. Their sole mandate is to provide education and support to family and friends who work face to face with individuals with a mental illness. In particular, they offer the 12-week Family-to-Family Education Course.

www.f2fontario.ca

NoStigmas Canada

The mission of NoStigmas is to raise awareness and erase the stigmas about suicide and mental illness by sharing stories of hope and inspiration, educating the general public about mental health, and helping those affected by mental illness. The driving force behind its mission is the Ally Program, a peer-to-peer, community-within-community support network developed by and for individuals affected by stigmas.

www.nostigmas.org

PeerZone Canada (excluding Ontario)
A peer-developed and peer-led resource that provides workshops, training and consultancy to support people with lived experience of mental distress or addiction to develop their roles in helping others. Operates in several countries (Australia, Canada, New Zealand, USA).

www.peerzone.info

PeerZone Ontario
A peer-developed and peer-led resource that provides workshops, training and consultancy to support people with lived experience of mental distress or addiction to develop their roles in helping others. Operates in several countries (Australia, Canada, New Zealand, USA).

www.peerzone.info

Schizophrenia Society of Canada
Provides information, education, support and advocacy for people with schizophrenia and their families.

www.schizophrenia.ca

England, Scotland and Wales
Carers Trust
National charity for, with and about carers. Provides support, information and services for carers throughout the UK. Provides access to local services.

www.carers.org

Carers UK
National charity for carers in the UK. Provides advice, information and support for all types of carers.

www.carersuk.org

Connect Support

A not-for-profit organization offering a comprehensive range of services to help and support carers and families of people with severe mental health problems in the Manchester region. Provides a range of carer support services (home visits, befriending carers, family interventions), carer support groups, education and training, and a volunteer scheme.

www.connectsupport.org

Hafal

Welsh charity for people with mental illness and their carers. Provides information, support, advocacy and services (e.g. help with housing, employment training, drop-in service) throughout Wales.

www.hafal.org

Living with Schizophrenia

Provides information on schizophrenia, including coping, recovery, symptoms and carer information.

www.livingwithschizophreniauk.org

Mental Health First Aid (MHFA) England/Scotland/Wales

Provides mental health training and research. Provides helpful guides for how to deal with particular mental health problems. Currently, over 25 countries have licensed and adapted the MHFA Australia program for their own settings, and more than three million people worldwide have been trained in MHFA skills.

England: https://mhfaengland.org

Scotland: www.smhfa.com

Wales: www.traininginmind.co.uk

Mental Health Foundation

Provides information, carries out research, campaigns and works to improve services for anyone affected by mental health problems.

www.mentalhealth.org.uk

Mind
National mental health charity that provides information, support, training and services across England and Wales.

www.mind.org.uk

National Mental Health Forum (Wales)/Fforwm Cenedlaethol Iechyd Meddwl (Cymru)
Provides a strong and diverse voice for people with mental health problems and carers throughout Wales. Foci include children, young people and families with mental health problems; mental health in the workplace and in later life; learning disabilities and mental health; influencing mental health policy decision-making throughout the UK; and research.

www.mentalhealth.org.uk

Rethink Mental Illness
Provides services, support groups and information on mental illness throughout England. Rethink's vision is for equality, rights, fair treatment and maximum quality of life for people affected by mental illness, their carers, family and friends.

www.rethink.org

Support in Mind Scotland
Provides support, information and services to people with mental illness and their families and carers. Their aim is to improve the quality of life of people with mental illness and their families, friends and supporters.

www.supportinmindscotland.org.uk

YoungMinds
The UK's leading charity advocating for children and young people's mental health and for those with a caregiver role.

https://youngminds.org.uk

Hong Kong SAR
Baptist Oi Kwan Social Service
A charitable organization providing a wide range of community services such as integrated children, youth and family services; pre-primary school; integrated elderly services; integrated mental health services; clinical

psychological and counseling services; and training and employment services. Also provides a comprehensive family mental health service, including caregiver support.

www.bokss.org.hk

Caritas Hong Kong
A charitable organization which offers a comprehensive selection of services, including integrated family service centers, psychology service, family aide, school social work service, and a range of services for people with substance use and mental health problems and their families.

www.caritas.org.hk

Christian Family Service Centre
A social service organization which provides a wide range of services, including child and family services, youth services, elderly care services, and for people with disabilities. Also provides a series of community mental health care services for people with mental illness and their families.

www.cfsc.org.hk

Hong Kong Family Welfare Association
Provides services to carers, family members and people with mental illness.

www.hkfws.org.hk

Hong Kong Mental Health Advocacy Association
Organization that provides information, training and support to families of people with mental illness.

www.familylink.org.hk

Mental Health Association of Hong Kong
Organization that provides information, support and community-based mental health services.

www.mhahk.org.hk

Mental Health First Aid (MHFA) Hong Kong
Provides mental health training and research. Provides helpful guides for how to deal with particular mental health problems. Currently, over 25 countries have licensed and adapted the MHFA Australia program for their

own settings, and more than three million people worldwide have been trained in MHFA skills.

www.mhfa.org.hk

New Life Psychiatric Rehabilitation Association
Non-government mental health organization that provides services for the recovery of people from mental illness. Also provides information and support to carers and families.

www.nlpra.org.hk

Parents/Relatives Resources Centre, Social Welfare Department
At present, the Hong Kong SAR Government operates 12 government-subsidized centers which provide community support for the parents and relatives/carers of persons with disabilities/mental illnesses.

www.swd.gov.hk/en/index/site_pubsvc/page_rehab/sub_listofserv/id_
supportcom/id_parentsrel

Richmond Fellowship of Hong Kong
International organization with community-based mental health services in Hong Kong.

www.richmond.org.hk

Tung Wah Group of Hospitals
A non-government organization which offers a wide spectrum of social welfare services. In particular, integrated service centers and family services provide services for the holistic development of young people aged 6–24 years, including individuals with substance use and mental health problems and families.

www.tungwahcsd.org/en/our-services/youth-and-family-
services;category/9

Ireland and Northern Ireland
A Lust for Life
A charity, which aims to support, inspire and empower people to take care of their own minds; change societal norms about mental health; and change societal infrastructure, so that "we always catch people where they fall."

www.alustforlife.com

Action Mental Health

Northern Ireland charity that works to enhance the quality of life and the employability of people with mental health needs or a learning disability in Northern Ireland.

www.amh.org.uk

CAUSE

A peer-led regional charity offering services to families, partners and friends throughout Northern Ireland caring for a loved one who has experienced serious mental illness. CAUSE is run by carers for carers, and offers a wide range of services, including a telephone helpline, support groups, activities and short breaks for carers, training for carers and professionals, carer support, and influencing services development and policy in local communities.

www.cause.org.uk

Family Carers Ireland

National voluntary organization that provides information, support and services for carers.

www.familycarers.ie

Grow

Mental health organization that provides information on mental illness and specializes in providing support meetings for people with mental illness.

www.grow.ie

Inspire

A charity and social enterprise with the aim of wellbeing for all. Provides mental health, learning disability, autism, addition and workforce wellbeing services throughout Ireland. Provides support services to people with mental health conditions, including supported housing, floating support services, advocacy services and community wellbeing services.

www.inspirewellbeing.org

Jigsaw

A national center for youth mental health. Aims to ensure that no young person feels alone, isolated and disconnected from others around them.

Provides support to young people with their mental health by working closely with communities across Ireland.

www.jigsaw.ie

Mental Health First Aid (MHFA) Ireland/Northern Ireland

Provides mental health training and research. Provides helpful guides for how to deal with particular mental health problems. Currently, over 25 countries have licensed and adapted the MHFA Australia program for their own settings, and more than three million people worldwide have been trained in MHFA skills.

Ireland: www.mhfaireland.ie

Northern Ireland: www.aware-ni.org/wellbeing-programmes/mental-health-first-aid

Mental Health Ireland

National organization that provides mental health information, support and services throughout Ireland. Aims to promote positive mental health and wellbeing to all individuals and communities in Ireland.

www.mentalhealthireland.ie

Mindwise

Northern Ireland charity for people with mental illness, their family and friends in Northern Ireland (formerly known as the National Schizophrenia Fellowship, then Rethink). Provides a broad range of services, including housing services, community resource centers and services, advocacy, employment and training services, carer support services, self-management program, mother and family wellness projects, and mental health and criminal justice-related services.

www.mindwisenv.org

Pieta House

Operates 15 centers throughout Ireland for people in suicide distress and those engaging in self-harm. Also provides free counseling, therapy and support to individuals, couples, families and children who have been bereaved by suicide.

www.pieta.ie

Recovery Self Help Method Ireland

A self-help, after-care charity which provides a specialized form of cognitive-behavioral training in self-help. Meetings are held regularly in various locations throughout Ireland.

www.recoveryireland.ie

Schizophrenia Ireland

The national organization dedicated to upholding the rights and addressing the needs of all those affected by schizophrenia and related illnesses, through the promotion and provision of high-quality services and working to ensure the continual enhancement of the quality of life of the people with the condition and their family and friends.

www.irishhealth.com/psg/menthealth2.html

Shine

National organization that provides mental health information, support and services throughout Ireland for people with mental ill health, their families and friends.

www.shineonline.ie

Turn2me Youth

In 2019, Turn2me.org and ReachOut Ireland joined forces to create Turn2me Youth, a space for young people, aged 12–18 years. The aim of Turn2me Youth is to make getting professional mental health support online as easy as possible for young people in Ireland.

https://turn2me.org/youth

Your Mental Health

The Irish Health Service Executive information and support portal with links to a broad range of information on mental health services.

www.yourmentalhealth.ie

New Zealand

Carers New Zealand

National carer organization that provides information, support, advice and education for carers.

www.carers.net.nz

Emerge Aotearoa

Provides care, support and a range of community services for people working towards mental health recovery.

www.emergeaotearoa.org.nz

Grow

Community-based organization that provides information on mental illness and specializes in providing support meetings for people with mental illness and their families.

www.grow.org.nz

Hearing Voices Network Aotearoa NZ

A charitable organization which is part of an international organization coordinated by Intervoice (www.intervoiceonline.org). Undertakes a broad range of activities, including information, research, resources, peer support groups, public awareness, events, workshops and training.

www.hearingvoices.org.nz

Kāhui Tū Kaha

A not-for-profit tribal support service, run by a Ngāti Whātua organization, providing housing, community mental health services, consumer advocacy, respite and residential mental health services, and rainbow services.

https://kahuitukaha.co.nz

Like Minds, Like Mine/Whakaitia te Whakawhiu te Tangata

A public awareness program funded by the New Zealand Government. The New Zealand Health Promotion Agency is the lead operational agency for the program. The program aims to increase social inclusion and end discrimination towards people with mental illness or distress, through public awareness campaigns, community projects and research.

www.likeminds.org.nz

Mental Health Foundation of New Zealand

Provides information, training and support on mental health and wellbeing issues.

www.mentalhealth.org.nz

Mind and Body
Part of the Emerge Aotearoa organization, but functions more or less separately providing peer support services. They provide mana-enhancing services that promote health and wellbeing for individuals, family, whānau (extended family) and communities.

https://mindandbody.co.nz

PeerZone
A peer-developed and peer-led resource that provides workshops, training and consultancy to support people with lived experience of mental distress or addiction to develop their roles in helping others. Operates in several countries (Australia, Canada, New Zealand, USA).

www.peerzone.info

Richmond New Zealand Trust
Non-government organization that provides community-based support services throughout New Zealand for people with mental illness and disability.

https://ageconcerncan.org.nz/listings/richmond-new-zealand-trust-limited

Supporting Families New Zealand
National organization that aims to support families, whānau and communities to foster mental wellbeing and plays a key role in the journey to wellness for people whose lives are affected by mental distress.

www.supportingfamilies.org.nz

South Africa
Cape Mental Health
Not-for-profit organization that provides or facilitates comprehensive, pro-active and enabling mental health services for people with mental health problems and their families, in the Western Cape and beyond. Provides a wide range of community-based programs and advocacy initiatives for the rights of people with mental illness and for mental health promotion, challenges the public stigma of mental illness, and strives to improve access to services.

www.capementalhealth.co.za

Cape Support Group for Mental Health

Provides a support group for families of people with prolonged mental illness, educates relatives and the community about mental illness, addresses community stigma towards people with mental illness, and works towards improving facilities for people with mental illness.

www.capesupport.org.za

Durban and Coastal Mental Health

An independent, not-for-profit, non-government organization. Works with people with mental health problems, families and communities by providing protective training workshops (work skills training, job creation initiatives), social work services, day and residential care, counseling and support, self-advocacy education and public mental health promotion.

www.dcmh.org.za

Mental Health Information Centre of South Africa

Provides the public and professionals with mental health information and an easy-to-use database of mental health professionals and organizations.

www.mentalhealthsa.co.za

South African Depression and Anxiety Group

South Africa's largest not-for-profit mental health and advocacy group. Provides a wide range of services, including, but not limited to, a network of over 200 support groups, counseling-and-referral call center, educational materials, workshops and training programs in communities, schools and workplaces.

www.sadag.org

South African Federation for Mental Health

South Africa's largest mental health organization. Provides mental health information for mental health care users, carers, mental health professionals and the media; national mental health awareness campaigns; empowerment and advocacy and referral; occupational wellness; and research.

www.safmh.org.za

South African Schizophrenia and Bipolar Disorders Alliance

A support group for people with schizophrenia, bipolar and related disorders and carers. Provides the following categories of support for people with schizophrenia, bipolar and related disorders and carers: (i) advice sharing and support, (ii) therapeutic activities and support, (iii) information on resources/facilities, and (iv) education and information sharing.

www.sabda.org.za

Ubuntu Centre South Africa

A not-for-profit organization focusing on human rights advocacy and building peer and mutual support networks for people with psychosocial disabilities.

www.ubuntucentre.wordpress.com

United States of America

American Association of Caregiving Youth

Organization that provides information, support and assistance to young carers.

www.aacy.org

American Psychological Association

The leading scientific and professional organization representing psychology in the USA. Their website contains a psychology help center, including a section on schizophrenia (www.apa.org/topics/schiz/index.html).

www.apa.org/helpcenter

Family Caregiver Alliance

Advocates on behalf of carers and provides services, information, programs, education and support to carers in the USA, with links to local services.

www.caregiver.org

Grow

Community-based organization that provides information on mental illness and specializes in providing support meetings for people with mental illness and their families.

www.growinamerica.org

Mental Health America

National community-based organization that provides mental health information, education and support, with links to local community services and programs.

www.mentalhealthamerica.net

Mental Health First Aid (MHFA) USA

Provides mental health training and research. Provides helpful guides for how to deal with particular mental health problems. Currently, over 25 countries have licensed and adapted the MHFA Australia program for their own settings, and more than three million people worldwide have been trained in MHFA skills.

www.mentalhealthfirstaid.org

National Alliance on Mental Illness

National grassroots organization that provides information, support and education on mental illness.

www.nami.org

National Institute of Mental Health

The lead federal agency for research on mental disorders. Their website also contains valuable information about mental disorders and sources of help for someone with mental illness (www.nimh.nih.gov/health/find-help/index.shtml).

www.nimh.nih.gov/index.shtml

NoStigmas USA

The mission of NoStigmas is to raise awareness and erase the stigmas about suicide and mental illness by sharing stories of hope and inspiration, educating the general public about mental health, and helping those affected by mental illness. The driving force behind its mission is the Ally Program, a peer-to-peer, community-within-community support network developed by and for individuals affected by stigmas.

www.nostigmas.org

PeerZone Georgia, USA

A peer-developed and peer-led resource that provides workshops, training and consultancy to support people with lived experience of mental distress or addiction to develop their roles in helping others. Operates in several countries (Australia, Canada, New Zealand, USA).

www.peerzone.info

PeerZone USA (excluding Georgia)

A peer-developed and peer-led resource that provides workshops, training and consultancy to support people with lived experience of mental distress or addiction to develop their roles in helping others. Operates in several countries (Australia, Canada, New Zealand, USA).

www.peerzone.info

Schizophrenia and Related Disorders Alliance of America (SARDAA)

Provides information, peer support and awareness of schizophrenia, and self-help group programs for people with schizophrenia and their families, in 31 states.

www.sardaa.org

Schizophrenia.com

Online community that provides in-depth information, education and support to people, carers and families affected by schizophrenia.

www.schizophrenia.com

Substance Abuse and Mental Health Services Administration

U.S. Department of Health and Human Services agency that leads public health efforts to advance the behavioral health of the nation and to improve the lives of individuals living with mental and substance use disorders, and their families.

www.samhsa.gov

Bibliography

Amaresha, A.C. and Venkatasubramanian, G. (2012) 'Expressed emotion in schizophrenia: An overview.' *Indian Journal of Psychological Medicine 34*, 1, 12–20. doi: 10.4103/0253-7176.96149

American Psychiatric Association (2013) *Diagnostic and Statistical Manual of Mental Disorders* (5th edn). Washington, DC: American Psychiatric Publishing.

Australian Government Department of Health (2012) *Mental health statement of rights and responsibilities.* Commonwealth of Australia. Accessed on 17/01/2020 at www.health.gov.au/internet/main/publishing.nsf/Content/mental-pubs-m-rights2

Baer, R.A. (2003) 'Mindfulness training as a clinical intervention: A conceptual and empirical review.' *Clinical Psychology: Science and Practice 10*, 2, 125–143. doi: 10.1093/clipsy.bpg015

Black Dog Institute (2012) *Factsheet: Treatments for depression.* Accessed on 03/02/2020 at www.blackdoginstitute.org.au/about-us/publications-and-resources/fact-sheets

Black Dog Institute (2013) *Depression explained.* Accessed on 17/01/2020 at www.blackdoginstitute.org.au/public/depression/depressionexplained/index.cfm

Cheng, G.L.F., Tang, J., Li, F., Lau, E. and Lee, T. (2012) 'Schizophrenia and risk-taking: Impaired reward but preserved punishment processing.' *Schizophrenia Research 136*, 1–3, 122–127. doi: 10.1016/j.schres.2012.01.002

Corstens, D., Longden, E., McCarthy-Jones, S., Waddingham, R. and Thomas, N. (2014) 'Emerging perspectives from the Hearing Voices movement: Implications for research and practice.' *Schizophrenia Bulletin 40* (Suppl. 4), S285–S294. Accessed on 03/02/2020 at https://doi.org/10.1093/schbul/sbu007

D'Zurilla, T.J. and Nezu, A.M. (2007) *Problem-Solving Therapy: A Positive Approach to Clinical Intervention* (3rd edn). New York, NY: Springer Publishing Company.

Early Psychosis Intervention (n.d.) *Dealing with psychosis toolkit (DWP).* Accessed on 03/02/2020 at www.earlypsychosis.ca/resources-and-downloads

Fuller Torrey, E. (2013) *Surviving Schizophrenia: A Manual for Families, Consumers and Providers* (6th edn). New York, NY: Quill.

Galanthi, G. (2008) *Caring for Patients in Different Cultures* (4th edn). Philadelphia, PA: University of Pennsylvania Press.

Headspace (n.d.) *Understanding self harm for families.* Accessed on 03/02/2020 at https://headspace.org.au/friends-and-family/what-is-self-harm-in-children

Jones, S. and Hayward, P. (2004) *Coping with Schizophrenia: A Guide for Patients, Families and Caregivers.* Oxford: Oneworld Publications.

Kitchener, B.A., Jorm, A.F. and Kelly, C.M. (2013) *Mental Health First Aid Manual* (3rd edn). Melbourne: University of Melbourne, ORYGEN Youth Health Resource Centre.

Kitchener, B.A., Jorm, A.F. and Kelly, C.M. (2015) *International Mental Health First Aid Manual*. Melbourne: University of Melbourne, ORYGEN Youth Health Resource Centre.

Lehrer, D.S. and Lorenz, J. (2014) 'Anosognosia in schizophrenia: Hidden in plain sight.' *Innovations in Clinical Neuroscience 11*, 5–6, 10–17. Accessed on 17/01/2020 at www.ncbi.nlm.nih.gov/pmc/articles/PMC4140620/pdf/icns_11_5-6_10.pdf

Lifeline (2010) *Tool kits: Carers of people with mental illness*. Accessed on 17/01/2020 at www.lifeline.org.au/Get-Help/Self-Help-Tools/Tool-Kits/Tool-Kits

Lopez, S.R., Nelson Hipke, K., Polo, A.J., Jenkins, J.H. *et al.* (2004) 'Ethnicity, expressed emotion, attributions, and course of schizophrenia: Family warmth matters.' *Journal of Abnormal Psychology 113*, 3, 428–439.

Luhrmann, T.M., Padmavati, R., Tharoor, H. and Osei, A. (2015) 'Differences in voice-hearing experiences of people with psychosis in the USA, India and Ghana: Interview-based study.' *British Journal of Psychiatry 206*, 1, 41–44. doi: 10.1192/bjp.bp.113.139048

MacCourt, P., Family Caregivers Advisory Committee, Mental Health Commission of Canada (2013) *National Guidelines for a Comprehensive Service System to Support Family Caregivers of Adults with Mental Health Problems and Illnesses*. Calgary, AB: Mental Health Commission of Canada.

Mayo Clinic (n.d.) *Mindfulness exercises*. Accessed on 03/02/2020 at www.mayoclinic.org/healthy-lifestyle/consumer-health/in-depth/mindfulness-exercises/art-20046356

McCann, T.V., Lubman, D.I., Gleeson, J., Crisp, K., Clark, E. and McCann, J. (2008) *Reaching Out. Supporting a Family Member or Friend with First Episode Psychosis: A Self-Help Guide*. School of Nursing and Midwifery, Victoria University and ORYGEN Research Centre, Department of Psychiatry, University of Melbourne, Melbourne.

Mental Health Association NSW (2010) *Caring for someone with a mental illness*. Accessed on 03/02/2020 at https://nnswlhd.health.nsw.gov.au/wp-content/uploads/Caring-for-Someone-with-a-Mental-Illness.pdf

Mental Health First Aid (2008) *Psychosis first aid guidelines*. Accessed on 03/02/2020 at https://mhfa.com.au/sites/default/files/MHFA_psychosis_guidelines_A4_2012.pdf

Mental Health First Aid Australia (2014) *Non-suicidal self injury: First aid guidelines*. Accessed on 17/01/2020 at https://mhfa.com.au/sites/default/files/MHFA_selfinjury_guidelinesA4%202014%20Revised_1.pdf

Mental Health First Aid Australia (2014) *Suicidal thoughts and behaviours: First aid guidelines*. Accessed on 17/01/2020 at https://mhfa.com.au/sites/default/files/mhfa-guidelines-suicide-revised-2014.pdf

Mental Health First Aid Australia (2019) *MHFA depression guidelines*. Accessed on 03/02/2020 at https://mhfa.com.au/sites/default/files/mhfa_depression-guidelines_sept2019.pdf

Mental Health Foundation (n.d.) *Hearing voices*. Accessed on 03/02/2020 at www.mentalhealth.org.uk/a-to-z/h/hearing-voices

Mental Health Foundation and the Princess Royal Trust for Carers (2010) *MyCare: The challenges facing young carers of parents with a severe mental illness*. Accessed on 17/01/2020 at https://professionals.carers.org/sites/default/files/media/mycare-report-final-5492.pdf

Mental Health Foundation Australia (n.d.) *Fight stigma*. Accessed on 03/02/2020 at www.mhfa.org.au/CMS/FightStigma

Michigan Department of Community Health (2011) *Combating stigma within the Michigan mental health system: A toolkit for change*. Accessed on 17/01/2020 at www.michigan.gov/documents/mdch/A_Toolkit_for_Change_403480_7.pdf

Mind (2016) *Understanding mental health effects of recreational drugs and alcohol*. Accessed on 17/01/2020 at www.mind.org.uk/media/5274202/understanding-drugs-and-alcohol.pdf

Mind (2016) *Understanding psychosis.* Accessed on 03/02/2020 at www.mind.org.uk/media-a/2949/psychosis-2016.pdf

Mind (2017) *How to cope when supporting someone else.* Accessed on 03/02/2020 at www.mind.org.uk/media-a/2903/supporting-someone-else-2017.pdf

Mind (2017) *How to support someone who feels suicidal.* Accessed on 17/01/2020 at www.mind.org.uk/media/5452271/how-to-support-someone-who-feels-suicidal-2017.pdf

Mind (2017) *Understanding schizophrenia.* Accessed on 03/02/2020 at www.mind.org.uk/media-a/2954/schizophrenia-2017.pdf

Mind (2019) *Depression.* Accessed on 03/02/2020 at www.mind.org.uk/media-a/2935/depression-2019.pdf

Mueser, K.T. and Gingerich, S. (2006) *The Complete Family Guide to Schizophrenia: Helping Your Loved One Get the Most Out of Life.* New York, NY: Guilford Press.

Multicultural Mental Health Australia (2004) *In Their Own Right: Assessing the Needs of Carers in Diverse Communities.* Parramatta, NSW: Australian Government Department of Health and Ageing.

National Institute of Mental Health (n.d.) *Schizophrenia.* Accessed on 17/01/2020 at www.nimh.nih.gov/health/publications/schizophrenia/index.shtml

New South Wales Consumer Advisory Group—Mental Health Inc. (n.d.) *Challenging stigma and discrimination.* Accessed on 18/01/2020 at https://old.being.org.au/challenging-stigma---discrimination.html

Nezu, A.M., Maguth Nezu, C. and D'Zurilla, T.J. (2007) *Solving Life's Problems: A 5-Step Guide to Enhanced Wellbeing.* New York, NY: Springer Publishing Company.

ORYGEN Youth Health (2017) *Helping someone with psychosis + young people.* Accessed on 18/01/2020 at https://oyh.org.au/sites/oyh.org.au/files/factsheets/OYH_helping_someone_psychosis_youngpeople.pdf

ORYGEN Youth Health (2017) *Psychosis + young people.* Accessed on 18/01/2020 at https://oyh.org.au/sites/oyh.org.au/files/factsheets/OYH_psychosis_youngpeople.pdf

ORYGEN Youth Health (2017) *Recovering from psychosis + young people.* Accessed on 18/01/2020 at https://oyh.org.au/sites/oyh.org.au/files/factsheets/OYH_recovering_from_psychosis_youngpeople.pdf

Queensland Government, Carers Queensland and FSG Australia (n.d.) *The YSCI young carers support tool kit.* Accessed on 18/01/2020 at https://carersqld.asn.au/services/young-carers-program

Reed, G.M. (2019) 'Innovations and changes in the ICD-11 classification of mental, behavioural and neurodevelopmental disorders.' *World Psychiatry 18*, 1, 3–19. Accessed on 18/01/2020 at https://onlinelibrary.wiley.com/doi/10.1002/wps.20611

Rethink Mental Illness (2013) *Factsheet: Hearing voices.* Accessed on 18/01/2020 at www.rethink.org/advice-and-information/about-mental-illness/learn-more-about-symptoms/hearing-voices

Rethink Mental Illness (2014) *Factsheet: Recovery.* Accessed on 18/01/2020 at www.rethink.org/advice-and-information/living-with-mental-illness/treatment-and-support/recovery

Rethink Mental Illness (2014) *Factsheet: Responding to unusual behaviour.* Accessed on 18/01/2020 at www.rethink.org/advice-and-information/carers-hub/responding-to-unusual-behaviour

Rethink Mental Illness (2014) *Factsheet: Supporting someone with a mental illness.* Accessed on 18/01/2020 at www.rethink.org/advice-and-information/carers-hub/supporting-someone-with-a-mental-illness

Romme, M.A. and Escher, A.D. (1989) 'Hearing voices.' *Schizophrenia Bulletin 15*, 209–216. Accessed on 03/02/2020 at https://doi.org/10.1093/schbul/15.2.209

Scanlan, M. and Manocki, H. (2005) *My journey to confidence*. Accessed on 18/01/2020 at www.mhtu.co.uk/intervention/manual-my-journey-to-confid.pdf

Schizophrenia.com (2005) *Tips for effectively communicating with a person who has schizophrenia*. Accessed on 18/01/2020 at www.schizophrenia.com/pdfs/communicate.pdf

Sekar, A., Bialas, A.R., de Rivera, H., Davis, A. *et al.* (2016) 'Schizophrenia risk from complex variation of complement component 4.' *Nature* 530, 177–183. doi: 10.1038/nature16549

Steel, Z., Marnane, C., Iranpour, C., Chey, T. *et al.* (2014) 'The global prevalence of common mental disorders: A systematic review and meta-analysis 1980–2013.' *International Journal of Epidemiology* 43, 2, 476–493. doi: 10.1093/ije/dyu038

Tanner, S. and Ball, J. (1989) *Beating the Blues: A Self-Help Approach to Overcoming Depression*. Sydney, NSW: Doubleday.

Thase, M.E. and Lang, S.S. (2004) *Beating the Blues: New Approaches to Overcoming Dysthymia and Chronic Mild Depression*. New York, NY: Oxford University Press.

Time to Change (n.d.) *Module 7. Stigma and discrimination: The facts*. Accessed on 03/02/2020 at www.time-to-change.org.uk/champions/e-learning/stigma-and-discrimination

Time to Change (n.d.) *Schizophrenia*. Accessed on 03/02/2020 at www.time-to-change.org.uk/about-mental-health/types-problems/schizophrenia

Voices Vic (n.d.) *A peer-led recovery program for people who hear voices*. Accessed on 03/02/2020 at www.unitingprahran.org.au/wp-content/uploads/2014/07/Managers-and-Clinicians-pack-13.11-complete-DO-NOT-MODIFY.pdf

Wehring, H.J. and Carpenter, W.T. (2011) 'Violence and schizophrenia.' *Schizophrenia Bulletin* 37, 5, 877–878. doi: 10.1093/schbul/sbr094

World Health Organization (2012) *Factsheet: Depression* (No. 369). Accessed on 18/01/2020 at www.who.int/mediacentre/factsheets/fs369/en

World Health Organization (2018) *ICD-11 International Classification of Diseases for Mortality and Morbidity Statistics (ICD-11 MMS)*. Geneva: World Health Organization.

World Health Organization (n.d.) *Lexicon of alcohol and drug terms published by the World Health Organization*. Accessed on 18/01/2020 at www.who.int/substance_abuse/terminology/who_lexicon/en

About the Authors

Terence V. McCann, RMN, RGN, Dip. Nurs. (Lon.), RNT, RCNT, BA, MA, PhD, is Adjunct Professor of Mental Health Nursing, Institute of Health and Sport, Victoria University, in Melbourne. He is also Honorary Professor, Turning Point, Eastern Health, in Melbourne. His clinical background is in mental health and medical-surgical nursing in England, Ireland and Australia. His principal research interests are prevention and early intervention with adolescents and adults in the mental health and substance use fields, and family interventions. He is passionate about improving outcomes for patients and their families. Terence has around 150 publications in peer-reviewed scientific journals, book chapters and reports and has given over a hundred major conference presentations.

Dan I. Lubman, MB ChB, PhD, FRANZCP, FAChAM, is a Psychiatrist and Addiction Medicine Specialist. He has worked across mental health and drug treatment settings in both the UK and Australia, and is currently Director of Turning Point, Australia's national addiction treatment, training and research center, and Professor of Addiction Studies and Services at Monash University. Dan's research is wide ranging, including the development of targeted telephone, online and face-to-face intervention programs within school, primary care, mental health and drug treatment settings, as well as building effective help-seeking and recovery responses. He is passionate about improving outcomes for patients and their families. He has published over 500 peer-reviewed scientific papers, major reports and book chapters, and is contacted regularly for policy advice and community comment.

Gayelene Boardman, RN, GDip (Psych. Nurs.), MHlthSci (Mental Health), PhD, is a senior lecturer in the College of Health and Biomedicine, Victoria University, in Melbourne. Her clinical background is in mental health nursing. She has worked in a variety of settings, including as unit manager of an acute inpatient unit, senior nurse in a community setting, senior crisis team clinician and nursing educator. From a research perspective, she is involved in mixed research methods in the areas of peer support, carer involvement and wellbeing, and undergraduate nurses' clinical practice.

Index

Other JKP Titles

Can't You Hear Them?
The Science and Significance
of Hearing Voices
Simon McCarthy-Jones

£13.99 | $19.95 | PB | 376PP | ISBN 978 1 78592 256 5 | eISBN 978 1 78450 541 7

The experience of "hearing voices," once associated with lofty prophetic communications, has fallen low. Today, the experience is typically portrayed as an unambiguous harbinger of madness caused by a broken brain, an unbalanced mind, biology gone wild. Yet an alternative account, forged predominantly by people who hear voices themselves, argues that hearing voices is an understandable response to traumatic life events. There is an urgent need to overcome the tensions between these two ways of understanding "voice hearing."

Simon McCarthy-Jones considers neuroscience, genetics, religion, history, politics and not least the experiences of many voice hearers themselves. This enables him to challenge established and seemingly contradictory understandings and to create a joined-up explanation of voice hearing that is based on evidence rather than ideology.

Simon McCarthy-Jones currently works as an associate professor in Clinical Psychology and Neuropsychology at Trinity College, Dublin and has over a decade of research experience regarding the topic of hearing voices.

Unlock Your Resilience
Strategies for Dealing with Life's Challenges
Stephanie Azri
Foreword by Rachel Kelly

£14.99 | $20.95 | PB | 192PP | ISBN 978 1
78775 102 6 | eISBN 978 1 78775 103 3

Resilience has never been more important in helping us navigate the stresses and adversity of modern life. Resilience acts as a protective armor that helps us deal with the toughest challenges that life throws at us. The best thing about resilience? It is a skill that you can develop at any age.

This book lays out 12 key skills that give you everything you need to unlock and develop your resilience, from self-esteem and self-care to emotional regulation and stress management. Each chapter supports skill development and includes exercises, activities and discussion topics as well as case studies from people who have used the program to improve their lives. Every key skill draws on various psychological techniques including CBT, positive psychology and solution-focused interventions.

The foundational skills this book teaches are ideal for anyone interested in improving their wellbeing, whether you are experiencing mental health issues or simply wish to increase your mental strength.

Stephanie Azri is a clinical social worker in the private, public and tertiary education sectors. She lives in Brisbane, Australia.

The Patient Revolution
How We Can Heal the Healthcare System
David Gilbert

£14.99 | $19.95 | PB | 272PP | ISBN 978 1 78592 538 2 | eISBN 978 1 78450 932 3

The NHS is in crisis—it is in record demand, and care services are at breaking point—but what if the solution to rescuing the NHS is in the hands of the patients themselves?

In this refreshingly positive and remarkable book, David Gilbert shares the powerful real-life stories of "patient leaders"—ordinary people affected by life-changing illnesses, disabilities or conditions, who have all gone back into the fray to help change the healthcare system in necessary and inspiring ways. Charting their diverse journeys—from managing to live with their condition, and their motivation to change the status quo, right through to their successes in improving approaches to health and social care—these moving and courageous stories aim to motivate others to take back control and showcase the pivotal importance of patients as genuine decision-making leaders.

Filled with hard-won wisdom and everyday heroism, *The Patient Revolution* challenges current discourse and sets out an empowering vision of how patient leaders can change the future of healthcare.

David Gilbert was the world's first Patient Director, at the Sussex Musculoskeletal Partnership, and is one of the pioneers of the concept of Patient Leaders. He is an expert in patient and public engagement at local, national and international levels, and has 35 years' experience working with the NHS.

Can I Tell You About Being a Young Carer?
A Guide for Children, Family and Professionals

Jo Aldridge
Illustrated by Jack Aldridge Deacon

£8.99 | $14.95 | PB | 56PP | ISBN 978 1 78592 526 9 | eISBN 978 1 78450 922 4

Meet Carly. Carly is a young person caring for her mother who has Multiple Sclerosis and depression.

Part of the best-selling *Can I Tell You About...* series, this book raises awareness about children who live with and care for parents or other relatives in the home. It describes what young carers like Carly do, and the practical and emotional impact caring can have on home and school life, both positive and negative. It also explains what support is available for young carers, including from family, friends and teachers as well as other professionals and online. Carly's story will help young carers explore their worries and concerns, and help family members and professionals support young carers.

Jo Aldridge is Professor of Social Policy and Criminology at Loughborough University. She is also Director of the Young Carers Research Group. Jo has published extensively in social policy, health and social care, specifically in the areas of children's rights, mental health and domestic violence.

Jack Aldridge Deacon is a postgraduate researcher at the University of Nottingham, UK and an illustrator.